PSYCHOMETRIC FOUNDATIONS AND BEHAVIORAL ASSESSMENT

To Lee Joseph Cronbach

PSYCHOMETRIC FOUNDATIONS AND BEHAVIORAL ASSESSMENT

Fernando Silva

SAGE Publications
International Educational and Professional Publisher
Newbury Park   London   New Delhi

Previously published by Ediciones Piramide, S.A., copyright 1989 (revised 1991), as *Evaluación Conductual y Criterios Psicométricos.*

For information address:

SAGE Publications, Inc.
2455 Teller Road
Newbury Park, California 91320

SAGE Publications Ltd.
6 Bonhill Street
London EC2A 4PU
United Kingdom

SAGE Publications India Pvt. Ltd.
M-32 Market
Greater Kailash I
New Delhi 110 048 India

Printed in the United States of America

Library of Congress Cataloging-in-Publication Data

Silva, Fernando.
    [Evaluación conductual y criterios psicométricos. Spanish]
    Psychometric foundations and behavioral assessment / Fernando
Silva.
      p. cm.
    Includes biblographical references and index.
    ISBN 0-8039-5266-X. — ISBN 0-8039-5267-8 (pbk.)
    1. Behavioral assessment. 2. Psychometrics. I. Title
BF178.5.S5513   1993
150'.72—dc20   93-7506

93 94 95 96 97 10 9 8 7 6 5 4 3 2 1

Sage Production Editor: Diane S. Foster

CONTENTS

FOREWORD

This is an important book. It fills, with great distinction, a need that has long existed in the assessment literature, a need for a detailed, rigorous, and searching examination of the relations between behaviorally oriented assessment and modern psychometric technology. Although the relations between these two approaches have been addressed by other authors, the present work is the first in-depth, book-length survey and critique of the issues involved. Further, it is the first such treatment to take full account of the newer developments and advances in psychometric theory.

Psychological assessment, in a meaningful and useful sense, got under way early in this century, with the development of intelligence tests. Later came personality, educational, and vocational tests. Concomitant with, and in a sense underlying, all of them was the development of certain statistical—that is, psychometric—procedures. In the 1960s a new thread, termed *behavioral assessment,* because of its emphasis on direct measures of subjects' behaviors, was added to the skein. Certain behavioral assessment theorists, in order to emphasize the uniqueness of their approach, tended to group together all other approaches under the label *traditional assessment*. Although this term had a certain appropriateness in the early days, it is no longer apt. For one thing, behavioral assessment itself has by now been around long enough to be called traditional. Further, all areas of assessment, including but not limited to behavioral assessment, have progressed greatly in recent decades, and the differences among them, as actually practiced, have become less sharp, although they still exist.

A crucial persisting question, which has been widely discussed in behavioral assessment circles, and which forms the basis of this book, is whether, and to what extent, psychometric concepts are relevant to research and practice in behavioral assessment. More specifically, the issues involved concern the pertinence to behavioral assessment of the concepts of method reliability, generalizability, and validity, and the uses of normative data. These concepts, it should be noted, were developed in the broader, test-oriented perspective, rather than in the behavioral assessment tradition, and the essential question is, Are such concepts meaningful for all kinds of assessment, including behavioral assessment, or, on the contrary, is the latter approach independent of such psychometric concerns?

Psychometric theory, although still based on its classical background, has, as noted above, undergone important advances in recent years. Behavioral assessment also has changed over the past 20 years—in particular, it is broader, more varied, and less rigidly circumscribed. Thus this is a highly opportune time to reevaluate the relevance of psychometric standards for behavioral assessment.

For the reader to consider these matters fairly and wisely, he or she must be fully informed, both on the current thinking in these matters in the behavioral assessment community and on the newer conceptions of psychometric theory. Professor Silva, with a foot in both camps, so to speak, is an excellent guide. He provides a detailed, balanced, and comprehensive review of the philosophical rationale of assessment from the behavioral perspective, and along with this he offers an extremely lucid and up-to-date account of the more expert thinking on psychometric methodologies. In particular, Silva's discussion of construct validity, especially in its relation to scientific method, is exemplary. It is also important to note that Silva does more than merely review the current scene; on the contrary, he presents strong, clear, and well-reasoned conclusions, all of which seem to me highly compelling.

One final note: It would be a serious mistake for prospective readers to consider this book meaningful only for workers in behavioral assessment. In fact, the book is relevant to the entire field of assessment, not only because behavioral assessment is, after all, a part of that broader scope, but because the book contains an excellent, very readable summary of newer advances in psychometrics. In brief, this volume is a major contribution to the assessment literature.

PAUL McREYNOLDS
University of Nevada

ACKNOWLEDGMENTS

I would like to thank Helio Carpintero, Lee J. Cronbach, Rocío Fernández-Ballesteros, and Carmen Martorell for their critical remarks on the manuscript; José Luis Pinillos for writing the Spanish Foreword; Lee J. Cronbach for his patience and painstaking efforts during the preparation of the English manucsript; and Paul McReynolds for writing the English Foreword and for his tireless and strong support of the publication of this book in the English language. Diane S. Foster, Nancy S. Hale, C. Deborah Laughton, Megan M. McCue, and Judy Selhorst from Sage's editorial staff are also kindly acknowledged.

INTRODUCTION

Disputes about the relation between behavioral assessment and traditional assessment, although heated throughout the former's birth and first developments, have diminished during the past several years. Although the topics touched upon in these debates were important, it could be said that such discussion is a purely typical phenomenon in the birth of new scientific disciplines that stress their opposition to what is already established and, to a great extent, classical.

Yet the truth is that the debates have recovered considerable vitality, at a time when one might think that behavioral assessment has already consolidated its development. Has this really happened? With respect to growth, it probably has, but not—in view of the many publications from the past decade—with respect to theoretical and practical identity (Bellack & Hersen, 1988). It seems that we are, today, witnesses to a profound "adolescent crisis" in behavioral assessment that requires that even the most basic questions be brought up again (Mischel, 1988). If this is so, out of the crisis will come a more mature identity that could develop along many different paths. What is in play is important for those who are interested in behavioral assessment and who have tried to aid in its implementation and diffusion.

The ultimate definition of this discipline will naturally have many facets. I am conscious that the most important facet is not the subject of review and reflection in this book. Adhering to the traditional canons, the substantive question is raised with respect to the *object,* that is, to what behavioral assessment proposes to study: in essence, the concept of *behavior* that, for all intents and purposes, we will adopt. Although in this volume I do not overlook questions about this concept, I am particularly concerned with problems of a *methodological* order that behavioral assessment must face, and the solutions to which, in one sense or another, must certainly have theoretical effects on the idea of behavior that will emerge.

Currently, a heated controversy separates, disperses, and even divides behavioral assessment specialists. The dispute obliges specialists to revise ideas and take positions. Clear examples of the conflict can be found in a speech delivered by R. O. Nelson (1983a) as president of the Association for the Advancement of Behavior Therapy and in an editorial by J. D. Cone (1987a) in the journal *Behavioral Assessment.* Likewise, in the most recent behavioral assessment handbooks, such as the second edition of the *Handbook of Behavioral Assessment* (Ciminero, Calhoun, & Adams, 1986) or the third edition of *Behavioral Assessment* (Bellack & Hersen, 1988), the most essential chapters have a controversial tone. It is also interesting to note that the book *Conceptual Foundations of Behavioral Assessment,* edited by Nelson and Hayes (1986a)—an essential work for understanding the current state of the discipline—focuses primarily on what could be called "the methodological question" and less on strictly conceptual subjects.

Given the inevitable dialectic between object and method, the resolution of this matter will affect the whole of behavioral assessment, in how it is understood and how it continues to develop. More than 10 years ago, in accepting José Luis Pinillos's gracious invitation to give two lectures during summer courses at the University of Santander (Spain), I addressed the methodological relations between behavioral assessment and traditional assessment (Silva, 1978), which is precisely where the current controversy is focused. It is now time to state it more completely and present it to other specialists for consideration and discussion.

At this time, it is necessary to mark out the issue more precisely. We already know that the nonjudgmental expression *traditional assessment—* which we should abandon—embraces too many things or, better said, too many approaches to psychological assessment. Among them, I shall concern myself only with what I feel is the main one: the *psychometric approach.* A good many writers identify the psychometric approach, broadly defined, with the totality of scientific psychological assessment. In turn, the nucleus of this psychometric approach resides in the so-called *test theory,* whose first developments go back to the beginnings of the century with Spearman and the theory of measurement error. During the evolution of test theory, norms for the construction, interpretation, and use of psychological measurement strategies and instruments became clearer. I shall speak of these as *psychometric standards.* The idea of reliability (directly related to measurement error) developed and, together with it, the concept of objectivity as intersubjectivity. Validity would later climb to the highest status, augmented by the practically oriented concept of utility. The derived, normative interpretation of scores accompanied these constructions, taking root, like the rest, in a differentialist perspective of psychological assessment. The relation of psychometric standards to behavioral assessment is the principal focus of this book; I concentrate on this relation in the discussion to the greatest possible extent.

Behavioral assessment, the origins of which are connected with some noteworthy developments of experimental psychology, did not begin with questions related to psychometric standards of quality as a primary concern. The methodological question that monopolized the attention of researchers for several years was that of internal validity of design, especially in single-case studies (e.g., Hersen & Barlow, 1976, 1984; Kazdin, 1982; Kratochwill, 1978; Sidman, 1960). I believe, however, that questions of internal validity cannot be answered adequately if the quality of exploratory instruments and strategies is not certain. It is essential to ensure the quality of the information collected with the instruments: the quality of observation, rating, or any other type of data. A careful reading of the references to this volume will illustrate that behavioral assessment has always been sensitive—although in multiple ways and with various emphases—to the question of metric standards of quality in behavioral undertakings. Consequently, psychometric standards have been its principal point of reference. Many pages have been filled with work on this subject. Nevertheless, until now it has not been dealt with in a reasonably complete and systematic way. To accomplish that is the first goal of this book. At the same time, however, let me say that from now on, I will also take a position on the behavioral/traditional controversy: I propose to defend the integration of the behavioral and the psychometric approaches, definitively reclaiming, so to speak, for the behavioral approach, the psychometric contribution. In short, the unification of these two approaches to psychological assessment is proposed as something required to resolve its theoretical problems and to make its practical interventions more effective.

A glance at the chapter titles will suggest how the topic is handled. After considerable rumination, I decided that it is not possible to treat psychometric standards of quality in behavioral assessment without reviewing, however rapidly, the concept of behavioral assessment from its origins to the present. Everything that follows stems from the first chapter, although much will be added to enrich the picture.

Chapter 2 aims to give a panoramic view of the topic of the book, where, among other things, the convenience of touching upon the issue of the idiographic approach in behavioral assessment is made clear. This is the subject of Chapter 3. Closely related to this subject, Chapter 4 addresses behavioral assessment and normative interpretation. Then we enter into an examination of classical psychometric standards. Chapter 5 reviews reliability and other related concepts. The more important question of validity requires more space. Above all, it seems necessary to present the psychometric concept of validity in detail as it is currently viewed by the experts. Chapter 6 deals with this. Later, the relations between behavioral assessment and each of its primary facets are reviewed: criterion-oriented validity in Chapter 7, content validity in Chapter 8, and, in more detail, construct validity in Chapter 9. In Chapter 10 the topic is utility, in its psychometric sense and with respect to behavioral assessment (which brings us to "treatment validity"). Finally, the book closes with some conclusions and thoughts on future developments that, beyond summarizing, present some synthesized reflections on the current meaning that the discussion of psychometric standards must obtain in behavioral assessment in order to be used at full power.

1

THE CONCEPT OF
BEHAVIORAL ASSESSMENT

The focus of this chapter is the concept of behavioral assessment, from its first developments to the complexities of its present role. Goldfried and Linehan quote a statement made by Johnson in 1946 that may well be considered a predecessor of behavioral assessment and that clearly demonstrates its inspiration:

> What the psychiatrist has to do . . . is to get the person to tell him not what he *is* or what he *was,* but what he *does,* and the conditions under which he does it. When he stops talking about what *type* of person he *is,* what his outstanding *traits are,* and what type of disorder he *has*—when he stops making these subject-predicate statements, and begins to use actional terms to describe his behavior and its circumstances—both he and the psychiatrist begin to see what specifically may be done in order to change both the behavior and the circumstances. (Johnson, 1946; quoted in Goldfried & Linehan, 1977, p. 18)

The date of this quotation notwithstanding, behavioral assessment is relatively recent when compared with psychological assessment in general and with clinical experimental psychology and, more precisely, with behavior modification and therapy. For example, we find no systematic discussion of behavioral analysis in Eysenck and Rachman (1965), Meyer and Chesser (1970), or Wolpe (1969). Yates (1975) noticed this need as he observed the great advances attained in only a few years:

> At the time *Behavior Therapy* was written . . . viable alternatives to psychiatric diagnosis were only beginning to be developed in detail, as is evident from the fact that only one small paragraph was placed appropriately in the final chapter on Future Trends. Now, only five years later, there would be no difficulty whatever in writing a whole book on the subject of behavior analysis. (pp. 36-37)

The 1970s saw the appearance of classical manuals, the first of which was *Diagnostik in der Verhaltenstherapie* (Diagnosis in Behavior Therapy), edited by Schulte in 1974. This decade also marked the beginning of the publication of specialized journals related to the field of behavioral assessment and, above all, a progressive increase in published works. This may also be seen in Prieto, Tortosa, and Silva's (1984) sciencemetric study of the aforementioned period.

Much has been written to justify the negligent attitude toward "traditional assessment" during the initial phases of the development of behavioral assessment. The most significant work in this respect is surely that of Goldfried and Pomeranz (1968). It is clear that this attitude was related to concrete theories and developments of psychodiagnostics of the time rather than to assessment as such. McReynolds (1986) reminds us of this when he quotes the introduction of Ullmann and Krasner's 1965 book, saying that there is indeed a place for psychological assessment in behavior modification. Two years earlier, in what is truly a pioneer text, Staats and Staats (1963) expressed this same idea in more detail:

> Perhaps a rationale for learning psychotherapy will also have to include some method for the assessment of behavior. In order to discover the behavioral deficiencies, the required changes in the reinforcing system, the circumstances in which stimulus control is absent, and so on, evaluational techniques in these respects may have to be devised. Certainly, no two individuals will be alike in these various characteristics and it may be necessary to determine such facts for the individual prior to beginning the learning program of treatment.
>
> Such assessment might take a form similar to some of the psychological tests already in use. It is possible, however, that a general learning rationale for behavior disorders and treatment will itself suggest techniques of assessment. (pp. 508-509)

This prescient remark was shortly followed by a truly programmatic publication by Kanfer and Saslow (1965) titled "Behavioral Analysis," a milestone in behavioral assessment (Fernández-Ballesteros, 1981c; Silva, 1978) and one of the principal instigators of the great subsequent expansion.

Nevertheless, the concept of behavioral assessment began to lose definition as time passed. Cone and Hawkins (1977a) pointed out that the term was in danger of losing a great deal of its intended value regarding the delimitation of assessment tools (see also Goldfried, 1977). Franks and Wilson (1980) likewise mentioned that behavioral assessment could expand to a point at which it would no longer have clear denotation or connotation. Mash (1979), on the other hand, noted that behavioral assessment was being spoken of more frequently with respect to what it is not than of what it is. It seems, he said, to have not a backbone but rather a series of characteristics; instead of precise limits, it offers a perspective on specific problems. The dominant tone of present-day authors (e.g., Bellack & Hersen, 1988) has been similar, as we will see in more detail further on. However, it seems that the moment has arrived in which to begin to clarify the concept's domain. Cone and Hawkins (1977a) indifferently interchange such expressions as *behavioral analysis, functional analysis,* and *behavioral assessment.* Other expressions could also be included: *behavioral diagnosis,* used in the work of Kanfer and Saslow in 1969, and *applied behavior analysis,* as defined by Baer, Wolf, and Risley a year earlier. I hope to shed light on the concept of behavioral assessment by analyzing these expressions later in this discussion.

Approaching the Concept

Undoubtedly, the expression least accepted has been *behavioral diagnosis,* owing to the strong psychiatric connotations or the "medical model" or "traditional" implications of the term *diagnosis.* Llavona (1984) therefore suggests that this expression not be used, because from a behavioral assessment point of view it would be inappropriate to assign subjects to predetermined treatments on the basis of specific symptoms or signs. Cone and Hawkins (1977a) however, accept the use of the aforementioned expression, whether it be in reference to pretreatment assessment (e.g., Silva, 1988) or to the final objective of assessment ("reaching a diagnosis").

Without a doubt, the matrix of the entire movement is in the *behavioral analysis* of Skinner and Ferster. The original meaning of this expression was blurred over the years through, it might be said, both overuse and defect. Overuse results from the fact that, in operant psychology, this expression tends to be used as a synonym for study and modification of behavior. Nothing limits it to questions of assessment. It should not be forgotten that, within operant psychology, the term *behavioral analysis* is identified with study and control of behavior. Much the same is to be said of its derivatives *applied behavioral analysis* and *functional analysis* (which we will deal with shortly). Defect, on the other hand, occurs for two reasons. First, behavioral assessment has for some time used explicative models that are complementary or alternative to the operant models that served as a base. Second, it was necessary to change the focus if behavioral assessment was to be talked about rather than behavioral analysis. This change came primarily from Baer, Wolf, and Risley (1968; also see Baer, Wolf & Risley, 1987) in their paper on applied behavior analysis. In this article, published in the first issue of the *Journal of Applied Behavior Analysis,* Baer et al. (1968) explain that they understand applied behavioral analysis as

> the process of applying sometimes tentative principles of behavior to the improvement of specific behaviors, and simultaneously evaluating whether or not any changes noted are indeed attributable to the process of application—and if so, to what parts of that process. In short, analytic behavioral application is a self-examining, self-evaluating, discovery-oriented research procedure for studying behavior. (p. 91)

Applied behavior analysis relates to social relevance and to applications in order to correct or improve unadapted behavior. The applied research concentrates on behaviors that are socially relevant and not on those that are more suitable for research. This likewise implies the study of behavior in a natural social environment rather than a laboratory setting (see also Hawkins, 1975). The essential criterion for the selection of independent variables must include the capacity to alter the behavior sufficiently to have social relevance (social impact, not solely a display of experimental control or statistical significance); on the other hand, the generalization of results will be the primary objective of the intervention. If the term *analytic* stresses the aspects of control and internal validation, then the term *applied* stresses social relevance in its various forms and with all its consequences.

The above-discussed work by Baer et al. (1968) had an enormous impact on the following decade (e.g., Garfield, 1978), above all in the field of behavior modification. The impact on assessment was relatively limited. It was not until the 1980s that this reorientation of behavioral analysis was generally brought to bear on tasks of assessment.

Another step toward clarifying the concept of behavioral assessment may be taken by defining the specifics of the expression *behavioral analysis.* Many times expressions have been used interchangeably, without putting sufficient emphasis on the need for *"functional" analysis,* although that need has been evident from the origins of operant psychology. This very point appears as the heart of Ferster's (1965) distinction between *functional analysis* and *topographic analysis*. Moreover, *functional analysis of behavior* was one of the expressions for which behavioral assessment became known as a discipline. We should then concentrate on it for a while.

Owens and Ashcroft (1982) point out that the expression *functional analysis* in psychology has precedents in other sciences. The physical-mathematical sciences employ functions to express systematic relations between variables without speculation about the metaphysical problems of causality. In the biological and social sciences, the role of functional analysis is to describe and explain a phenomenon in relation to its function or utility within a system. In the latter meaning we can clearly see the functionalist roots of behaviorism, which emphasize this role of *functional* in the study of behavior (remember the distinction between *functional* and *topographic*).

Owens and Ashcroft (1982) further observe that these two meanings, distinct yet related, have been integrated into psychology. *Functional analysis* makes reference to both the detection of variables that affect a phenomenon and the manner in which this is done: "Psychology, interestingly, provides an elegant framework for the combination of these applications [of the term *functional*], concerned as it is with both the determinants of behaviour and the form of the relationships between such determinants and behaviour" (p. 182).

Within the realm of behavioral assessment, several authors have offered definitions or descriptions of a functional analysis of behavior. For some, as in the cases of Peterson (1968) and Fontaine and Ylieff (1981), this involves a variety of tasks, from systematic observation of target behaviors in order to obtain a baseline to the analysis of therapeutic developments and their far-reaching effects. However, with such a broad interpretation the concept seems to lose connotative value. On the other hand, all the authors reviewed agree generally with what Skinner (1938, 1953) understood as functional analysis of behavior: that the fundamental part of a functional analysis is that cited above from Owens and Ashcroft (see also Bijou & Peterson, 1971; Fernández-Ballesteros, 1981c; Fernández-Ballesteros & Vizcarro, 1984; Mash & Terdal, 1974; Wiggins, 1973). Owens and Ashcroft (1982) further state:

> A functional analysis approaches a problem or a phenomenon seeking to answer questions regarding the function of the phenomenon to the system as a whole and the form of the relationship between this phenomenon and the function(s) it serves. The production of such analyses is on the basis of information regarding what has come to be known as the ABC paradigm, i.e.

investigation of the behaviour (B) its antecedents (A) and its consequences (C). It is suggested that attempts to analyze a phenomenon which omit any of these factors are likely to produce incomplete analyses. (p. 188)

Limiting the concept gains clarity and precision, but does not reduce it to a simple task. Some classic and didactic texts may have given a false impression of simplicity to which Kanfer and Saslow's (1965) proposed model was already a counterpoint.

A complete functional analysis of behavior requires an *empirical* demonstration of the relationships between criterion attributes of behavior and the environmental conditions which control them. Such a demonstration requires, at a minimum, that reliably observed or recorded attributes of behavior (frequency, intensity, duration) exhibit lawful relationships with *experimentally manipulated* aspects of the stimulating environment. (Wiggins, 1973, p. 376)

At the same time, Haynes (1983) reminds us that the most complex stage of behavioral assessment is surely the unification of incoming data from distinct research strategies into one comprehensive functional analysis; that is to say, an "integrated conceptualization of targeted behaviors, their determinants, and mediational variables" (p. 412; see also Haynes, 1990, 1991; Peterson, 1968).[1]

The functional network is usually complex, involving motor and physiological as well as cognitive behavior, behavioral chains that may contain true R-R (or $R = S - R$) functional relationships, behavioral covariants that may be understood as response classes, an extensive consideration of the involved stimulus variables ranging from single stimuli to sociocultural norms, and so on.[2] Therefore, it is necessary to accept functional analysis as a complete research method that involves the formation and testing of hypotheses as well as the formulation of models. This idea is further emphasized by Owens and Ashcroft (1982), who insist that a functional analysis need not agree with any theoretical formulation, so long, I would add, as one does not continue into therapeutic planning, where it appears to be impossible to avoid formulation in terms of theory. Thus it is understandable that a functional analysis, in all its complexity, may be put into practice less often than some imagine (Hawkins, 1986; Haynes, 1988; Nelson & Hayes, n.d.) and may rarely be understood or researched (Haynes, 1983, 1988, 1990, 1991).

The use of the expression *behavioral assessment* in behavior modification and therapy was not common until the mid-1970s. The definition offered by Nelson and Hayes (1981) is representative: "Behavioral assessment is the identification and measurement of meaningful response units and their controlling variables (both environmental and organismic) for the purposes of understanding and altering human behavior" (p. 3; see also Hayes, Nelson, & Jarrett, 1986; Nelson, 1987; Nelson & Hayes, 1979a,

1979b, n.d.). However, this concise definition does not give an idea of the heights the concept may reach, and it overlooks several possibly controversial questions, some of which are discussed below.

Controversial Issues

First of all, authors give a different emphasis to behavioral assessment in works that go beyond pretreatment assessment. Some authors refer only to the pretreatment procedure (e.g., Kanfer, 1972; Lanyon & Lanyon, 1976; Schulte, 1974), and the concept is then characterized by such tasks as the following: identification and measurement of target behaviors; identification and measurement of preceding events, concomitants, and consequences; functional analysis, which leads to the development of an explanatory model of the problematic behavior; investigation of the treatment plan, taking into account both patient and environment, determination of a baseline, and establishment of goals and design of strategies for the individualized treatment.

However, the majority of authors note that the tasks of behavioral assessment also apply throughout the treatment program as well as in the follow-up analysis. This follow-up would extend to examination of obtained results, including generalization effects. This expansion of the concept, introduced by Cautela (see e.g., Dickson, 1975), is emphasized by several authors who view the evaluation of treatment as "one of the major defining characteristics and strengths of behavior assessment" (Hartmann, Roper, & Bradford, 1979, p. 17).

No one denies the importance of appraising treatment effects. Indeed, it should not be forgotten that one of the factors that motivated the development of behavioral assessment as a part of behavior therapy was the need to contrast and evaluate results empirically. The fact that some authors seem not to count assessing the effects of treatment within the concept of behavioral assessment may indicate their view that tasks dealing strictly with evaluation should be left out. Authors who include the evaluation of treatment in the definition of behavioral assessment are forced to subordinate "evaluation" to "assessment" (e.g., Hartmann et al., 1979). The confusion about the relation between assessment and evaluation in psychology is well known, and this is not the place to elaborate on what may be more than a matter of semantics. The expression *behavioral assessment* will attain its maximum extension if the terms *assessment* and *evaluation* become synonymous, which is fairly probable.

There is an alternative to this dilemma: maximum reduction of the domain denoted by *behavioral assessment*. This is what Cone (1987a) has proposed:

> Minimally, behavioral assessment can be seen as the objective description of specific human responses. . . . The qualifier "minimally" is intended to show

that behavioral assessment includes activities that carefully document the occurrence of behavior and some dimensional quantity thereof, even though they might not include a complete functional analysis. Thus, a careful description of eating responses in field settings (e.g., fast-food restaurants) could qualify as behavioral assessment even if it did not include the determination of environmental controls over those responses. In this sense, behavioral assessment can be seen to be an important part of, but not synonymous with behavior analysis. The later is the more inclusive term, and requires the former. (p. 2)

It is clear that Cone's view is diametrically opposed to the views of many authors. No one denies that behavioral assessment contains an important descriptive component, at the beginning of the process and throughout its different phases and tasks. The observation that a complete functional analysis is complex and not always carried out in self-denominated "behavioral analyses" is also captured above. But these thoughts have little to do with the attempt to reduce behavioral assessment to descriptive elements. In the works of almost all authors examined, functional analysis is not simply a task of behavioral assessment, but rather its *central task.* "The fundamental objective of behavioral assessment," writes Fernández-Ballesteros (1981c) "is to determine the conditions which control the problem behaviors" (p. 89), since this is the task that leads to the design of therapeutic programs, through the formulation of hypotheses and the postulation of working models. Saying this, Fernández-Ballesteros does not depart from the line set by Skinner (1953) himself "for what may be called a causal or functional analysis" (p. 25). This is also the core of the close relationship between diagnostics and treatment claimed by behavioral assessment, whose fundamental function is to present useful information for the elaboration and implementation of intervention programs, without which behavioral assessment would make no sense.

Even though Cone presents his proposed definition with the qualifier "minimally," it cannot be accepted. The objective description of responses is *one* of the tasks of behavioral assessment. If we were to stop there, we surely would not be able to speak appropriately about it (nor about psychological assessment or psychodiagnostics). A functional analysis is also one of the tasks of behavioral assessment; although its central one, functional analysis is a less connotative concept than that of behavioral assessment. It forms a part of the latter and not the reverse. Not to include functional analysis within behavioral assessment would be to disregard both an essential component of the overall concept and the development of the discipline from its very beginnings until now.

Other attempts at reduction bear on the kinds of variables to be examined. Some authors (following the orthodox line of thought about behavioral assessment peculiar to operant psychology) limit it to publicly observable behavioral events. The following two definitions are examples:

> In its most narrow sense, behavioral assessment describes a philosophy of measurement and associated methodologies for constructing useful information about persons, based solely on some dimension(s) of publicly observable act of an organism in interaction with its environment. (Kanfer, 1979, p. 37)

> Behavioral assessment is defined . . . as assessment done by researchers, clinicians, and other practitioners whose goal is to measure aspects of people's overt, publicly observable behavior, rather than covert, private events or constructs like thoughts, attitudes, or personality attributes. (R. R. Jones, 1977, pp. 331-332)

To emphasize further the exclusion of subjectivity, Jones compares behavioral assessment with "non-behavioral assessment," which measures "thoughts, attitudes, opinions, traits, *and* unverifiable behavior." According to Jones, these types of assessment should remain separate.

Nevertheless, these opinions seem to represent poorly both the collective opinion of theorists, researchers, and practitioners of behavioral assessment and the development of this discipline. In the first place, Jones makes the not uncommon mistake of putting subjective activities, such as thoughts and opinions, on the same level as personality traits and attributes—concepts that are usually tied to theoretical positions in the psychology of personality. The desire to exclude the latter type of variable from the discipline is virtually unanimous among behavioral assessors. The reverse is true of the former. It is appropriate here to cite Mischel (1968): "In the present view [of social learning theory], cognitions, affects, and other mediating events are construed as internal responses that also serve as stimuli, linking external stimulus inputs with the ultimate overt terminal outputs in complex stimulus-response chains (Berlyne, 1965)" (p. 300). Even authors known to take a more radical position assume a broad definition of behavior that "include[s] private as well as public events" (Cone, 1987a, p. 2). Peterson (1968) had already pointed out that "the behavior is enacted by a person, and not all the behavior of persons is explicit and observable" (p. 35), and Kanfer (1979) had said that to exclude subjectivity is to consider behavioral assessment "in its most narrow sense." He himself put this question into historical perspective:

> The last decade of work in behavioral assessment has led to some doubt that measurement of unambiguously defined observable response classes will suffice for a full account of human behavior in the social context. The future task of behavioral assessment therefore lies in an expansion of measurement

instruments and of theory to encompass both dependent and independent variables of greater complexity than those with which behavioral assessment has dealt in the past. (p. 39)

As a matter of fact, what we detect now is rather "an expanding focus" in behavioral assessment. Haynes (1990), from whom I take that expression, adds:

The array of variables, functional relationships, and target behaviors included in behavioral construct systems is expanding. There is an increased focus on behavioral chains, temporally extended and noncontiguous determinants, predictor and mediating variables, community and environmental settings, cognitive and physiological variables, treatment generalization, side-effects and social systems. (p. 446)

We will soon deal with some of these remarks, but let us come back now to Kanfer's remark on the expansion of measurement instruments (see also Haynes, 1991).

The urge to expand the range of measurement instruments is not at all new (in spite of vigorous protest from Barrett, Johnston, & Pennypacker, 1986; see also Haynes, 1990, 1991). Wolpe, in 1958, already emphasized the advantages of the self-report and the interview when measuring and classifying anxiety responses (e.g., Fernández-Ballesteros, 1981c, 1983a). Although Bellack and Hersen (1988) assert that "the label 'behavioral assessment' is not useful if behavioral and non-behavioral assessors alike use the same procedures" (p. 614), a look at the tables of contents of manuals on behavioral assessment or, more directly, at the recent dictionary of behavioral assessment techniques by Hersen and Bellack (1988a) makes evident the recent enormous expansion of instrumentation. Moreover, empirical studies show that it is characteristic not only of academics, but also of professional practitioners (among others, see Emmelkamp, 1981; Hersen, 1988; Nelson, 1981). On the other hand, Bellack and Hersen (1988)—applying an observation already made by Peterson (1968)—note that no *via regia* of instrumentation exists because direct observation of behavior has also been seriously questioned. This idea is expanded upon by Haynes (1990, 1991), Suen and Ary (1989), and Barrios (1988) in his criticism of the so-called direct methods (e.g., Cone, 1981a). All this matter is not exempt from problems, among which is the theoretical base of instruments, which we will see later. But it helps significantly to restrict the scope of "unverifiable behavior" mentioned by Jones and to strengthen the expansion of the field of action, demanded by the great majority of behavioral assessors. We should not forget the following remark by Skinner (1953): "The line between private and public is not fixed. The boundary shifts with every discovery of a technique for making private events public" (p. 282).

Let us return to the variables that are considered the focus of analysis. The expansion developed primarily in the cognitive approach, to the extent that cognitive variables in the conceptualization of behavioral problems as well as in behavioral intervention have been increasingly included. Their use varies from causal antecedent factors to contingencies of problem behavior, or mediational variables in treatment outcomes in the form of causality attributions or of expectations (Haynes, 1983, 1991; see also Bellack & Hersen, 1988; Fernández-Ballesteros, 1981b). It is possible that this "cognitive invasion" has surpassed acceptable limits (see, for instance, Haynes, 1990; Wolpe, 1989) by having escaped all metric or empirical control. In this sense, Fernández-Ballesteros (1986) opposes, with reason, Landau and Goldfried's (1981) use of the concept of scheme. Fernández-Ballesteros points out other abuses of the cognitive-behavioral models, especially the danger of identifying environment with perceived environment. These are examples that must be kept in mind and that suggest the maintenance of the scientific frame as long as this frame implies objectivity, at least as a synonym of intersubjectivity. Nevertheless, nothing prevents the consideration of ideas and perceptions or, more generally, subjective variables within such limits.

The move toward subjectivity has not been the only expansion. Focusing exclusively on one problematic behavior in assessment and intervention now seems erroneous (Plaum, 1982). Extending the thought of Kanfer and Saslow (1965), Kanfer and Nay (1982) point out that premature concentration on one goal often leads to the overlooking of other important areas. In the planning phase of the process of assessment, several questions and levels of analysis should be considered in order to avoid giving undue attention to objectives that may seem very apparent, but that, at the same time, may not contribute much to solving the client's problems (see also Barrios, 1988; Bellack & Hersen, 1988). At the other extreme of the assessment process, so to speak, a decidedly broader perspective than the traditional one arises:

> Measuring the success the treatment has had is, of course, dependent upon how we define success. Behavior therapists do not yet agree with one another on what are acceptable outcome criteria for the common problems (e.g., Mash, 1985). Behavior therapists do, however, agree with one another that change in an isolated target response of an isolated individual in an isolated setting at an isolated time is not an acceptable treatment outcome. For a treatment to be successful, there must be some spread of therapeutic effects to nontreated responses, nontreated persons, nontreated settings, or non-treated points in time. (Barrios, 1988, p. 16)

Thus the expansion of the points of interest goes in many directions. For example, it is repeatedly emphasized that consideration of the environmental influence on behavior must respect and attempt to detect all its complexity (e.g., Rogers-Warren & Warren, 1977). Consequently, "to study contextual variables will require a broadening of our units of analysis in both space and time" (Dumas, 1989, p. 421).[3]

Concerning the expansion of the temporal focus within which events should be taken into account, Haynes (1990), remembers that "behavior analysts presume, often without empirical justification, that a greater proportion of variance in the parameters (e.g., probability, magnitude, duration) of behavior disorders can be attributed to current rather than historical behavioral-environmental variables" (p. 426). And he adds in another recent work that "an exclusive focus on contemporaneous phenomena and relationships may limit the validity and application of behavioral construct systems" (Haynes, 1991, p. 434). This is why he recommends, together with other authors, a "*systems* view of persons and behavior disorders" (see also Evans, 1986).

On the other hand, emphasis is placed on an aspect that is no less relevant: the consideration of R-R relationships. The "ghosts" related to traditional theoretical models of personality, especially those of trait psychology, still seem to be frightening (Evans, 1986). Yet, it is the case that the relationship of responses and their subsequent assessment has been important. This is because of the interest that may be created by the existence of covariance among topographically distinct responses or the existence of responses that are organized in hierarchies of probability, because of the proven precedence of response chains over determined behaviors, the functional value of some as prerequisites of others, and finally because the modification of determined responses may be associated with desired or undesired changes in other responses (Evans, 1986; Voeltz & Evans, 1982). All of this, as Nelson and Maser (1988) successfully point out, may be maintained within classical explanatory behavioral schemes. It is worth taking a look at what Haynes (1983) derives from the effects of these remarks for behavioral assessment:

The implications for the theoretical bases and methods of behavioral assessment are far-reaching. Reliable demonstrations of such behavioral interrelationships would suggest that: (1) it is difficult to account satisfactorily for behavioral variance through reference only to situational factors, (2) multimethod/multisituation/multitarget assessment is needed for a comprehensive functional analysis and for a comprehensive evaluation of treatment effects, and (3) examination of response chains and hierarchies may facilitate the derivation of valid and useful functional analyses, and treatment plans. Behavioral interrelationships must themselves be considered a dependent variable that is under the control of other variables. It is apparent that some responses covary while others do not, that hierarchies may be reliable or unreliable, that behavioral interrelationships may vary across developmental stages, situations, responses, and individuals. (p. 418; see also Haynes, 1991)

With the above in mind, it is obviously important to integrate individual differences (e.g., Haynes, 1991) and, beyond, *personality* in behavioral assessment. Few authors explicitly recognize this integration, although, in fact, many are taking it into account, in the same way as "the implicit acceptance of response structures is abundantly evident" (Evans, 1986, p. 131). Special worth is given to texts such as the prologue of the main behavioral assessment manual edited in Spain:

> Finally, the analysis of behavior . . . is instead dependent on the entire organism; that is to say, the subject's personality. In short, a complete behavioral assessment cannot be reduced to stimuli and responses, rather it must also encompass processes and personality. (Fernández-Ballesteros & Carrobles, 1981a, p. 12)

Does this renounce a behavioral approach and make senseless the expression *behavioral assessment*? Yes, if traditional, substantialist conceptions of personality are assumed; but that is not obligatory. The suggestive interpretation of Wallace (1966) defines personality in terms of skills or capacities of learned responses, in terms of "response repertories." The idea was reused by Peterson (1968). According to Staats, "basic behavioral repertories" constitute personality in a behavioral interpretation, and they, together with the stimulating situation, have causal value in the determination of responses. Perhaps this author is the most relevant in the attempt to integrate a behaviorist conception with the study of personality (see Staats, 1975, 1980, 1986; Staats & Fernández-Ballesteros, 1988). But this integration seems possible only from a focus different from that of radical operant behaviorism. In a 1986 personal communication cited by Carbonell (1987), Staats was emphatic in his appraisal: "What is not generally understood is that radical (in other words, operant) behaviorism did not even offer a conceptual foundation for the development of the field of behavioral assessment."

This statement, which may seem extreme, is not far from reality. It is not only that the force of operant behaviorism, so important in other fields, may never have been very successful in behavioral assessment. It is also true that one has the impression that the developments of behavioral assessment, or at least the major portion of those developments, occurred in spite of operant behaviorism and by assaulting its principles. This impression is related to diverse fields already touched upon above, linked to the kinds of variables to be considered and also to the instrumental resources it must count on (on self-reports, see Staats & Fernández-Ballesteros, 1987). Staats (1986), defending paradigmatic behaviorism as a coherent and more solid theoretical base for behavioral assessment, shows how one can avoid excessively narrow models and still maintain a behavioral perspective.

The last part of the preceding paragraph touches upon something that has been evident for several years: There are diverse models, or paradigms, within behavioral psychology. For Fernández-Ballesteros and Carrobles (1987), the coexistence of a strict behaviorist (operant) focus, a social behaviorism focus, and the different variants of the cognitive movement derived from social learning theory is primarily responsible for the crisis that exists today in behavior therapy and in behavioral assessment. Mischel expresses these in an almost dramatic form. Commenting on a book by Nelson and Hayes (1986a), he says that "all the authors agree that behavioral assessment is in trouble, but they disagree greatly about just what the trouble is, the reasons for it, and the solutions. Most important, they disagree about what behavioral assessment is and should be" (Mischel, 1988, p. 125). And Barrett et al. (1986) say that "behavioral assessment now accepts a state of definitional-methodological anarchy" (p. 166).

In fact, the diversity of models has become more apparent in the past decade, and the tendency toward monographic publications proves it (e.g., Kendall & Hollon, 1981). Any attempt to describe the present state of behavioral assessment must surely encompass an enormous diversity of micromodels, lines of work, strategies, instruments, and assessment practices that are not fully formed in defined theoretical models. The researcher who has probably examined the state of things most thoroughly is Cone—also through his own theoretical evolution. The central idea in a 1986 publication by Cone is that "there is not one behavioral assessment; there are many" (p. 126). Theoretically, according to Cone in 1986, the possibility exists of the very reasonable summary of 32 models, taking into account these possibilities: if the scientific approach is inductive or deductive, if the assessment can be defined as idiographic or nomothetic, if it focuses on the study of behaviors or traits, if interest is shown in intrasubject or intersubject variability, and, finally, if the emphasis in the environmental area can be defined as interactive or noninteractive (see Cone, 1986, fig. 4-1). However, all this diversity and its possible heuristic value are gone from Cone's more recent work. In spite of its title (which speaks of "multiple models of behavioral assessment"), Cone (1988) reduces the possibilities to two opposing models, a distinction he polarizes and radicalizes. The models are the "nomothetic-trait" and the "idiographic-behavior" approaches, defined as follows:

[The *nomothetic-trait approach*] can be characterized as selecting traits or syndromes (e.g., social anxiety, depression, agoraphobia) as its subject matter, developing instruments to assess them deductively, and establishing the adequacy of such instruments in terms of variation in scores between individuals on them. The instruments are then used to evaluate the effects of independent variables in formal research with groups of subjects or to evaluate interventions applied to individuals.

The contrasting strategy will be referred to as the *idiographic-behavior approach.* It can be characterized as selecting specific behavior as its subject matter, developing procedures to assess it inductively, and establishing the adequacy of such procedures in terms of variation in scores within individuals on them. (Cone, 1988, pp. 46-47)

This latter-day polarization, artificial and unnecessary, loses much of the force of Cone's ideas. Still, one can see that the term *nomothetic-trait approach* defines very well what has come to be called the traditional approach. Therefore, it is not surprising that Cone shows a clear preference for the idiographic-behavioral strategy; in the end, this is the only behavioral approach that he adopts. Nevertheless, opposing it to the traditional approach makes it lose much of its applicability (see, e.g., Cone, 1988, box 2.1, on the application of psychometric concepts to both approaches). In an attempt to simplify, Cone creates two entities that seem to leave the effective reality of behavioral assessment untouched.

Finally, let us briefly address the relation between behavioral assessment and behavior therapy. The appearance of behavioral assessment and a good part of its development have been and continue to be at the heart of behavior therapy. Authors agree on that, and yet their opinions differ. Franks and Wilson (1978) express a traditional opinion in which *behavioral assessment* and *behavior therapy assessment* (Mash & Terdal, 1974) should be considered synonymous: "Assessment is an integral part of the process of behavior therapy and such specialization is constructive only as long as this is kept in mind" (p. 167). Barrios (1988) is more forceful:

Behavioral assessment is not and never has been a discipline separate from the discipline of behavior therapy. . . . The close ties between the two disciplines are due to behavioral assessment having arisen out of the behavioral approach to clinical treatment in order to meet the special needs of clinical treatment (e.g., Hersen & Barlow, 1976; Nelson, 1983[a]). Simply put, it is because we have a behavioral approach to clinical treatment that we have a behavioral approach to clinical assessment and not vice versa. Behavioral assessment's *raison d'être* is behavior therapy, and its motto, if it had one, would be *Ad Serviam.* (pp. 3-4)

It is logical from this point of view to distrust any proposal of behavioral assessment as a discipline separate from its matrix and to regard that possibility as a danger (Franks & Wilson, 1980).

Other authors have the opposite opinion. Fernández-Ballesteros and Carrobles (1981a) point out that behavioral assessment should not be reduced to a subdiscipline within behavior therapy, because its field of application is much broader. For Schaller and Schmidtke (1983), behavioral assessment can be applied toward different goals from those of therapeutic modification and can be "conceived as a general process in the presence of many problems" (p. 490). McReynolds (1986), in turn, points out that although the bonds between behavioral assessment and behavior therapy are very strong, the techniques of behavioral assessment are increasingly applied to nontherapeutic contexts and to the study of important theoretical questions. Because of this, he foresees an increasing independence of behavioral assessment from its therapeutic roots.

The narrower the conception of behavior therapy, of course, the less possibility there is of including behavioral assessment within it; and, in particular, the relationship between the concepts of behavior therapy and behavior modification plays a role here. On the other hand, if behavior modification implies limitless behavioral intervention, it is difficult to find a broader field for behavioral assessment. Nevertheless, the foremost question seems rather to be whether behavioral assessment is necessarily validated by the results of the intervention, that is, whether the results of treatment are conclusive for deciding on the quality of a functional analysis. I have addressed this question elsewhere in more detail, stating that the execution of intervention programs also depends on aspects other than pretreatment assessment (Silva, 1988). Thus it does not seem reasonable to impose treatment outputs as a necessary and sufficient criterion for assessment validation. In this way, an unsound "immunization" of intervention strategies from the necessary hypothesis-testing process is avoided as well (Westmeyer, 1975).

Conclusions

This chapter has concentrated on both the concept of behavioral assessment and some of the current issues surrounding that concept. The expression *behavioral assessment* has taken on a comprehensive character that engulfs expressions such as *behavioral diagnosis* (Kanfer & Saslow, 1969) and, in a sense, *applied behavior analysis* (Baer et al., 1968). In accordance with the majority of authors specializing in assessment, and in spite of what Cone (1987a) has said, it is concluded that functional analysis of behavior falls within behavioral assessment (not the reverse) and, as is known, represents the central task of pretreatment assessment: to devise an investigation that leads to hypotheses concerning the functional ties between the targeted behavioral variables and those that, according to some functional psychological model implying learning, determine them. Should *behavioral assessment* refer to tasks that go beyond pretreatment assessment and perhaps imply evaluation of results? That question remains open; the answer will depend on the relations the scientific community constructs between the concepts of *assessment* and *evaluation.*

The most recent historical evolution speaks clearly in favor of expanding behavioral assessment in several directions: regarding the targets of study (no longer limited to directly observable motor behavior, but rather encompassing both the physiological and subjective areas), regarding the techniques of compilation of information (no longer limited to observational or automatized recording, but rather including a wide range of procedures), regarding the consideration of the environmental aspect, regarding the types of relationships between variables (for example, the increasing attention to R-R relationships), regarding the explicative models used, regarding the temporal periods included in the explicative scheme, and so on.

Naturally, all this expansion has put the identity of behavioral assessment in danger. Some authors say that the identity has been lost, that perhaps it no longer makes sense to talk about behavioral assessment, or that there is no such thing as one behavioral assessment but rather that there are many. This current situation has recently revived the polemics and positions of behavioral assessment theorists. In my opinion, it is possible to assimilate all the sensible expansions of the concept while preserving the identity of behavioral assessment. This identity is understood to lie in behavioral assessment's main task—to provide the necessary information for the design of treatment programs—and in the way this task is approached, that is, by carrying out a functional analysis of behavior that leads to the formulation of a working model of the behavior in question.

Notes

1. At this level, difficulties in the practice of functional analysis are mentioned by, among others, Nelson (1988; see also Haynes, 1988; Haynes & O'Brien, 1988). Haynes views functional analysis as so complex that it seems very difficult to do. However, technical assistance—for instance, in the form of personal computers—could make a valuable contribution (see Repp et al., 1989).

2. It is interesting to note that along this same line, correlational analysis has been conveniently placed within the framework of functional analysis of behavior (e.g., Wahler & Fox, 1981).

3. I cannot expand, at this point, on the interesting results that the interaction between "environmental psychology" and "behavioral psychology" have produced, and continue to produce, with immediate impact in the field of assessment. Along with the book cited (Rogers-Warren & Warren, 1977), Cone and Haynes's 1981 book and the recent revision of Martens and Witt (1988) may also be consulted.

2

BEHAVIORAL ASSESSMENT AND PSYCHOMETRIC STANDARDS
An Introduction

P sychological assessment in one form or another has never been inattentive to the development of behavioral assessment. As an introduction to this chapter, we shall take a brief look at opinions expressed about behavioral assessment and psychometric standards by specialists who cannot precisely be included within this movement.

It was quickly understood that behavioral assessment, born of a paradigm different from that of current psychological testing, should likewise go through different courses of development. In 1969, Arthur pointed out that the behavioral model of assessment leaves the decision about treatment to the individual clinician, ignoring theories that base decisions on taxonomy and testing. Its development in the experimental approach would have left out completely the correlationally obtained information. McReynolds (1971) concisely expresses a justification for that omission: "The concepts of reliability and validity are part and parcel of the attribute model," and therefore "are not wholly applicable to other models" (p. 6; see also Fernández-Ballesteros, 1979, 1980). However, a noticeable change from these remarks in the second volume of McReynolds's *Advances* appears six years later in the fourth volume:

> Although behavioral assessment techniques are in some respects quite different from the more traditional evaluative methods employed in personology and clinical practice, the similarities between the two orientations are much greater than the differences. Both approaches deal with similar practical problems—such as anxiety, depression, and social skills—and with such common problems of measurement as standardization, reliability, validity, and utility. (McReynolds, 1977, p. 3).

Fiske (1978), who discussed differences between the orientations on a number of occasions, noted also about the same time that "behavioral assessment looks more and more like traditional measurement" (p. 363). Finally, in the 1980s, the opinion that behavioral and psychometric assessment are coming together is common among specialists in psychological assessment. This is expressed, for example, by Weiner (1983) and Lanyon (1984), who adds, "although no marriage should be expected." Anastasi (1985) summarizes the idea as follows:

> Another clinical area that began in an antitesting mood and has moved toward the recognition of psychometric standards is that of behavioral assessment. Because of the rapid growth of behavior therapy and behavior modification programs, the development of assessment techniques to meet the needs of these programs has lagged far behind at the outset. Makeshift procedures and crude techniques were prevalent. Many practitioners, moreover, regarded behavioral assessment as fundamentally irreconcilable with the traditional psychometric approach. In the 1970s, however, several leaders in behavior therapy presented thoughtful and convincing arguments demonstrating that behavioral assessment must meet traditional psychometric standards with regard to standardization of materials and procedures, normative data, reliability, and validity. And some progress has been made in implementing these goals in the development of special procedures suitable for behavioral assessment. (p. xv; see also Anastasi, 1988)

Up to this point, we have the panorama, so to speak, as seen "from outside" behavioral assessment. Now the question is, How is it seen "from inside," by its own authors?

The Movement Toward the Integration
of Psychometric Standards

The initial rejection clearly dealt with instrumentation, which was completely, or almost completely, useless for the tasks and aims of behavioral assessment. In this sense, books by Peterson and by Mischel, as well as an article by Goldfried and Pomeranz, all published in 1968, had a great impact. Staats (1975), among others, addressed the same idea later. But the problem was broader and deeper. Staats (1975) brought us back to the origins: "Skinner's rejection of the concepts, methods, and instruments associated with traditionally oriented psychometrics, in favor of direct behavior observation, has had a growing influence" (p. 424). The deterministic and experimental basic model, contradictory to a probabilistic and correlational alternative, produced an adamant rejection of statistical methodology (e.g., Bayés, 1978; Sidman, 1960). 1 It is not strange, therefore, that the rejection extended to psychometric standards. Another of Goldfried's articles (Goldfried & Kent, 1972), to be discussed in Chapter 9, had an even greater impact than his 1968 work.

Nevertheless, soon after, there also appeared claims for the psychometric contribution. In the same year Goldfried and Kent published their article, Kanfer (1972) pointed out the danger of sacrificing scientific precision and declared himself in favor of standardizing instruments in order to avoid the "excessive individualization of procedures that permit no comparisons across treatment populations or clinicians" (p. 419). Based on survey data, Kanfer concluded that behavioral assessment was going through a period that bordered on chaos: Instruments were being hastily made and used, without any scientific evidence to support their utility.

Similar concerns were expressed throughout the 1970s. Wiggins (1973) mentioned "from outside" that functional exploration and the postulation of models usually occurs "on the basis of highly fallible measures" (p. 376). Johnson and Bolstad (1973) noted that the precision, reliability, and validity of the data used in behavior modification is often unknown or inadequately established. At the same time, they emphasized the different types of biases that affect those data. Goldfried pointed to the proliferation of instruments together with the great lack of psychometric development. He noted the parallel to the development of projective techniques in the 1940s. He believed there was a danger that history may repeat itself and that once again a sort of rustic assessment would prevail; therefore, he argued for a great concern about validation (Goldfried, 1981; Goldfried & Linehan, 1977). The same parallel was referred to by Hartmann et al. (1979), who quoted a text by Rabin on the projective techniques that could be a warning. Hartmann et al. defended the usefulness of norms and of studies on reliability, validity, and utility in behavioral assessment. Complaints about lack of psychometric development were repeated by Leitenberg (1978), Curran (1978), Fernández-Ballesteros (1979), and O'Leary (1979), who called attention to the deficiencies in the psychometric training of any behavioral assessor who would be content with "face validity."

During the 1980s, the voice of concern was still frequent and forceful. For example, Franks and Wilson (1980) insisted that behavioral assessment instruments were deficient with respect to standardization, validation, and norming, even though some of them already had a decade or more of clinical use. Kanfer and Nay (1982) interestingly observed that behavioral assessors who had shown so much interest in replicability and validity (internal validity designs) of intervention procedures had, on the other hand, neglected the quality of the information that is the basis for the study of such procedures. With this in mind, they recalled Sundberg (1977), for whom "the same general psychometric concepts and principles apply to behavioral measures as to any other; the APA standards for tests (1974) need to be studied by behaviorists, too" (p. 168).

Along the same line, Bellack and Hersen (1988) have recently reminded us that

> objectivity, reliability, and validity are fundamental to any sound assessment approach. . . . The reliability, validity, and utility of any procedure should be paramount, regardless of its behavioral or nonbehavioral development. We see no value in reifying behavioral strategies just because they are behavioral if they are not psychometrically sound and clinically useful. (p. 614)

The same insistence appears in the work of Martínez Arias (1981), Evans and Wilson (1983),[2] Kendall (1984), Ciminero (1986),[3] Barrios and Hartmann (1986),[4] and Haynes (1983, 1990, 1991),[5] among others. Authors such as Mischel (1985) express the same concern.

Often we see the inclusion of a greater dedication to psychometric issues in "future developments" or "future directions" of behavioral assessment. Kanfer's 1972 article emphasized this, and it was among the "questions which are still unanswered" listed by Goldfried and Sprafkin (1974). Among the future issues Goldfried wrote of three years later (Goldfried, 1977; Goldfried & Linehan, 1977) are the comparison of the validity of traditional and behavioral procedures, studies of difficulty levels, and the push toward standardization. The same ideas appear in Goldfried's later work also (see Goldfried, 1979); some of them are developed in detail among "future perspectives" in one paper (see Goldfried, 1981). At the same time, Franks and Wilson (1978) suggested further development of measurement instruments with statistical and methodological sophistication as well as greater consideration of test theory. For the future, Fernández-

Ballesteros (1979) proposed an increased experimental and psychometric base for both the construction of new instruments and the evaluation of those already in existence.

In the 1980s, writers were also ready for historical recapitulation of these topics. For example, Strosahl and Linehan (1986), who began by recognizing how behavioral assessment had opened up with respect to traditional developments over the previous years, attempted to explain the major points of separation. On the one hand, strict requirements for metric quality in behavioral assessment seem to have been premature, if we consider the fact that it is a young field, still rather undisciplined and devoid of common standards. On the other hand, the roots and the basically academic development of behavioral assessment pushed it within the "publish or perish" dynamic, making thorough studies, replications, and cross-validations difficult, and putting behavioral assessment in constant danger of separating investigation from application. The high costs and difficulties in the application of many behavioral assessment techniques also contributed to this danger. Several authors were aware of this some time ago (e.g., Emmelkamp, 1981; Ford & Kendall, 1979; Swan & MacDonald, 1978; Wade, Baker, & Hartmann, 1979). From another point of view, this also suggests an integration of psychometric procedures into behavioral assessment.

There are more substantive issues, however:

> The once firm conviction that extensive and rigorous empirical scrutiny would firmly establish the validity of various behavioral assessment proce-dures has given way to a more gloomy and pessimistic appraisal. Perhaps the most pessimistic stance is that human behavior is so internally disorganized and situation-specific that little or no relationship should be expected be-tween measures of the same target behavior, systems of behavioral respond-ing, or similar behaviors occurring in different situations. Although there is food for thought in such assumptions, this approach seems dangerously close to "throwing the baby out with the bath water." In this case, the bath water is a plethora of unreplicated and/or unreplicable research findings which are interpreted to mean that human behavior is so idiographically determined that nomothetic measurement is nearly impossible. Rather than explaining this prob-lem as a result of some annoying attributes of human behavior, perhaps we should examine publication and academic policies which promote an unbridled expan-sion of research instruments without a concomitant focus on providing the basic validation data which could guide investigators in the selection of appropriate assessment methods. (Strosahl & Linehan, 1986, p. 15)

When considered in perspective, observations such as these fit into a historical evolution that seems to have moved from an initial detachment of behavioral assessment from psychometrics toward a progressive, clear approach. In effect, this is what Goldstein and Hersen (1984) humorously mention: "Looking at behavioral assessment today from an historical perspective, it certainly appears as though the 'baby' is being returned from the discarded bath water" (p. 12; see also Hersen, 1988). Kendall also noted this in his 1984 revision. Haynes (1983) stated that development had resulted in rapid improvement in the quality of the instruments used. He undoubtedly expressed this historical perspective best. To conclude this point, let us consider the following lengthy quote from Haynes (1983):

> In the early stages of the behavior therapy movement, behavior analysts developed and applied many assessment instruments that were derived intuitively, rather than empirically (Haynes, 1978). Many were applied without being subjected to prior psychometric evaluation. Questionnaires on fear, assertion, depression, social skills, life history, and marital and family interaction and satisfaction, as well as observation-coding systems were used without regard to psychometric parameters such as reliability and validity. The result was the dissemination and application of assessment instruments of dubious criterion, content, and construct validity. . . .
>
> This disregard for psychometric principles was probably based on five factors: (1) the necessity of applying assessment instruments at a time when empirically validated, behaviorally oriented instruments were not available; (2) an assumption that the applicability of psychometric principles was limited to instruments developed within traditional trait construct systems; (3) an excessive reliance on face validity of behavioral assessment instruments; (4) a lack of training of behavior analysts in psychometric principles and procedures; and (5) a rejection of most assessment instruments associated with traditional clinical paradigms. A number of authors (Goldfried, 1979; Cone & Hawkins, 1977[a]; Haynes, 1978; O'Leary, 1979) have reflected on the problems associated with the use of non-empirically based assessment instruments and have recommended increased attention to psychometric factors. Psychometric evaluation of behavioral-assessment instruments is a necessary component in establishing confidence in the validity of inferences drawn from them.
>
> Recently, behavioral-assessment instruments are being constructed and refined using more empirically grounded approaches such as discriminant function analysis, analytic-synthetic models, contrasted-groups comparisons, and population sampling (Conger et al., 1980; Freedman et al., 1978; Lahey, Vosk, & Habif, 1981; McFall, 1982; Mullini & Galassi, 1981; Twardosz et al., 1979). . . .
>
> Increased attention to other psychometric factors in behavioral assessment has also been evident in the past several years. Examples include studies examining the factor structure of questionnaires (Galassi & Galassi, 1980), the concurrent validity of observation measures (Haynes, Follingstad, & Sullivan, 1979; Robin & Weiss, 1980), the concurrent validity of interview measures (Haynes et al., 1981) and role-play measures (Bellack et al., 1979;

Wessberg et al., 1979) and the reliability of measures used in behavioral medicine (Russo, Bird, & Masek, 1980). Further examples include examinations of the sensitivity of psychophysiological measures of female sexual arousal (Henson, Rubin, & Henson, 1979), the accuracy and external validity of self-monitoring (Dericco, Brigham, & Garlington, 1977; Hay, Hay, & Nelson, 1977), and the sources of variance in a variety of assessment instruments (Baum et al., 1979; Hayes & Cavior, 1980; Haynes & Horn, 1982). (pp. 414-415; see also Haynes, 1991)

The Opposite Movement:
Pyschometric Standards Are Rejected

The situation is not as clear as the preceding paragraphs and citations would suggest, because of the existence of contrary opinions. The movement toward psychometric assessment has never, in reality, been accepted by all behavioral assessors. Although, in her opinion, classical procedures used in traditional assessment to ensure reliability and validity of the instruments apply to behavioral assessment, Fernández-Ballesteros, in her 1979 work, pointed out the heated debate that was developing over this. Eight years later, Fernández-Ballesteros made the same observation (Fernández-Ballesteros & Carrobles, 1987): A group of specialists increasingly criticized the application of psychometric principles to behavioral assessment. In part because of this, the third edition of her manual had to be modified.

Although these critics are undoubtedly in the minority, they seem to be very important. Their foremost defenders are well known: R. O. Nelson and J. D. Cone. The importance of these critics comes not only from their prestige among behavioral assessors, but also from the strength and appeal of their argument. All of this suggests the need for an expanded discussion.

A chronological review of Cone's works reveals a radical change in attitude. At the beginning he showed himself a decided defender of applying psychometric procedures in behavioral assessment. His 1976 paper states that classic psychometric procedures cannot be applied automatically to the data of a behavioral assessor, and that important philosophical-conceptual differences exist. Despite this, the paper deals with applying Campbell and Fiske's (1959) multitrait-multimethod strategy to behavioral assessment by means of multicontent-multimethod-multibehavior matrices. This would require analysis of group data and the adoption of the concept of reliability or, better yet, the adoption of the generalizability approach of Cronbach, Rajaratnam, and Gleser (1963) and Cronbach, Gleser, Nanda, and Rajaratnam (1972). The application of this approach is further clarified and broadened in an article of the following year titled "The Relevance of Reliability and Validity for Behavioral Assessment" (Cone, 1977b). Cone strongly defended their importance and exhibited a decided tendency to combine the psychometric standards and behavioral assessment. The differences, which would be more philosophical than methodological, influence the differential emphasis given to concrete exploration strategies or universes of generalizability.

The scenario changes completely one year later, when Cone (1978b) states that traditional psychometric procedures are not applicable to behavioral assessment, given that they were created to deal with constructs or traits and to examine interindividual differences. Cone states that "classical test theory is inextricably bound up with these interests," and he goes so far as to conclude that "it is difficult to think of instances in which traditional, inter-individual psychometric procedures would have any value for behavioral assessors. Select any such procedure and examine what it tells us" (p. 16).

Cone maintains this same line of thinking during the 1980s. In a 1981 work (see also Cone, 1987b), he argues that "a truly behavioral view of assessment is based on an approach to the study of behavior so radically different from the customary individual differences model that a correspondingly different approach must be taken in evaluating the adequacy of behavioral assessment procedures" (Cone, 1981b, p. 51). Cone tries to show that traditional standards of quality, specifically, reliability including the theory of generalizability, are inappropriate or irrelevant for studying the behavior of individual subjects or single cases. In a later work with Hoier dealing with "the radical behavioral perspective" in child assessment (Cone & Hoier, 1986), Cone insists on rejecting classical psychometric procedures and standards. (Surprisingly, Cone himself uses such procedures extensively in research on a "template matching" technique that is included in the same work.) In short, Cone doubts the supposed utility of the traditional psychometric concepts, insisting that utility "will have to be demonstrated convincingly with each application" (1987a, p. 2).

Unlike Cone, R. O. Nelson has basically maintained the same posture over the years. In 1977, she questioned the importance of reliability and validity in behavioral assessment defended in Cone's early works (Nelson, Hay, & Hay, 1977). Specifically, she deemed the use of dimensions of generalizability unnecessary, and said that weak generalizability along some dimension should not imply imprecision of the data: "The assessment tool may be precise, but the behavior being measured may have changed" (p. 428). Further, generalizability theory would have some other problems, for example, the problem of using random samplings rather than step-by-step replication studies, which would seem much more suitable in behavioral assessment research.

In 1979, Nelson took a more moderate position. In the first article of the journal *Behavioral Assessment,* she states that psychometric procedures and those of generalizability can be applied to the data that behavioral assessment techniques generate, even though "the assumptions underlying these procedures often do not apply" (Nelson & Hayes, 1979b, p. 10). Moreover, she suggests that behavioral assessment ought to move toward the increased use of multivariate statistics and research on the generalizability of assessment, especially in relation to criterion situations (Nelson & Hayes, 1979a).

She was again more radical by 1983, in her address as president of the Association for the Advancement of Behavior Therapy (Nelson, 1983a) and in another paper (Nelson, 1983b). In a recapitulation of events, she detects a period of great disillusionment at the beginning of the 1980s. This disillusionment with behavioral assessment reflects an unsatisfactory psychometric development of behavioral assessment techniques. According to Nelson, the discontent arises from a great misunderstanding that needs to be unraveled. Construction of standardized assessment techniques and thus of a standard set or battery of instruments has been frustrating.

The standardization of procedures, as already mentioned, seems to be an old aspiration of behavioral assessment, noted as far back as Kanfer (1972) and repeated in the works of authors such as Hartmann et al. (1979), Mash and Terdal (1981), Mash (1985), and Kratochwill (1985). Dickson (1975), however, rejects that aspiration in a text that deserves attention:

> It may be that this trend toward standardization of behavioral assessment techniques . . . is contradicted by the essence of behavioral theory. If one assumes that each target for assessment represents a single experiment, then what is needed is the scientific method of experimentation and research, rather than a formalized schedule for assessment. Whether the target represents a unit of behavior for a single organism or for a total community, the experimenter can apply the rules of experimental evaluation to that target with great flexibility. Within this framework, each situation is seen as unique, and the reliability of the approach is not a function of standardization techniques . . . but rather is a function of following the experimental method in evaluation. (pp. 376-377)

If the requirements for standardization are extended further and the construction of a battery of instruments of universal application is intended, then the rejection becomes broader. Kanfer (1972) himself pointed out that behavioral assessors "do not think that a universal test-battery is in sight or even desirable at this time" (p. 420). Several years later, Fernández-Ballesteros and Carrobles (1987) again say that such a battery would be contradictory to a behavioral model. Returning to Nelson, it is here—more than in the question of standardization as such—that she focuses criticism. Although she supports the construction and use of a set of behavioral assessment instruments (Nelson, 1983b), "there never will be nor should there be a standardized behavioral assessment battery, especially one based on psychometric criterion. Waiting for a behavioral version of the IQ test-MMPI-Rorschach test battery is like waiting for Godot" (Nelson, 1983a, p. 198). Such a battery does not seem possible in Nelson's opinion, not only because it would require infinite techniques in order to assess different response systems of many abnormal behaviors, in different situations, and through different methods of assessment, but above all because "the use of psychometric criteria to select behavioral assessment techniques is generally antithetical to behavioral theory" (p. 199).

In subsequent publications, Nelson sticks to the idea that psychometric theory including generalizability does not provide an adequate base to appraise the quality of behavioral assessment. Even though limited contributions are occasionally generated from these approximations, the above is the central argument. But why do they not provide this base? Nelson (1983b; see also Hayes et al., 1986), in the wake of classic expositions in behavioral assessment (e.g., Mischel, 1968; Peterson, 1968), groups the differences into three areas, detailed below.

1. *assumptions about behavior*

In psychometric theory, an observed score is a composite of the true value plus measurement error. The true score is a hypothetical entity, which is typically assumed to be enduring and stable because it reflects an enduring, stable, internal entity. Reliability and validity assess the consistency of measurement. Rather than an event to be explained, consistency is viewed as the hallmark of a good assessment device. If the true score is assumed to be consistent, then consistent measures are thought to be less contaminated by error and more reflective of the true score.

It is an assumption of behavioral assessment, however, that behavior is not necessarily enduring and consistent. Inconsistency in measurement may only be produced by actual changes in behavior and not only by an imprecise behavioral assessment technique (Nelson, Hay & Hay, 1977). When low reliability or validity coefficients are obtained, behavioral assessors ask, "Is it the measure or the behavior?" (Cone, 1981[b], p. 55). Thus, consistency or inconsistency is an empirical fact to be explained, not an inside route to quality measurement. The behavioral question becomes, What are the variables responsible for the degree of consistency seen?... There is no assumption of "measurement error." ... "Error" has no place in behavioral theory.

In most situations, it does not seem appropriate to expect consistency in responding, given the assumptions of behavioral theory. Since behavior is assumed to be modifiable (often rapidly so), test-retest reliability should not necessarily be expected. Since behavior is assumed to be situation-specific, concurrent validity across assessment situations should not be routinely predicted. Given the assumption that responses are distinguished by the functions they serve, inconsistency across response systems is not surprising. While the results of psychometric investigations of behavioral assessment techniques have been disappointing to some, in fact, the results have simply verified the assumptions underlying behavioral assessment. Thus, when inconsistency across situations, responses, or time is found, it is not necessarily a statement about the quality of behavior assessment. It is, instead, an empirical fact requiring explanation. (Hayes et al., 1986, pp. 471-472)

2. *level of analysis*

A second reason why psychometric and generalizability theory may not be an appropriate criterion for evaluating behavioral assessment is that their levels of analysis differ. Psychometric research is almost universally based on the analysis of group data, while behavioral assessment emerged from the intensive analysis of individuals. The issue is not one of number (few vs. many) but of the level of analysis (individual vs. group) upon which principles and findings are based. (Hayes et al., 1986, p. 472; see also Barrett et al., 1986)

3. *models of causality*

The third reason that psychometrics and generalizability theory may not provide adequate criteria for evaluating the quality of behavioral assessment is that the two perspectives differ fundamentally in their view of causality. In psychometrics, events can be explained based on the structure of the organism (e.g., the structure of the mind). That is, structure can assume causal status. In modern behaviorism, the structure of the organism is itself something to be explained by the functional interaction between the organism and the world over both short time frames (e.g., in the lifetime of the individual) and long time frames (e.g., in the lifetime of the species). Structure is not unimportant in this view, but it is not a cause. Instead it is a host for causal agents.

The philosophical source of disagreement in this area is what we take to be a "cause." Modern behaviorism evaluates causes in terms of our abilities to predict and to control (and to understand, which relates to the breadth and depth of prediction and control). The difficulty with structural "causes" is that they can sometimes help us predict, but as long as we stay inside the structure we cannot know how to control. Demonstration of control involves manipulation. Manipulation of a structure must be initiated from outside that structure. Thus, structuralistic "causes" (whether they be called behavior, bodily states, traits, or cognitions) cannot serve the functions required of causes in modern behaviorism. As a structural approach, psychometrics can provide data to be evaluated functionally, but cannot functionally evaluate data, including those derived from behavioral assessment. (Hayes et al., pp. 476-477)

Underlying these observations is the old conflict between structuralism and functionalism (Nelson & Hayes, 1986b). The behaviorist movement has leaned decidedly toward the latter. As a result, Nelson (1983a) insists that behavioral assessment procedures and strategies be functionally, rather than structurally, evaluated—that is, based upon their objectives and goals. The primary function they serve, at least in the assessment of pretreatment status, is to supply information useful in intervention. Hence their ultimate worth will be based on the contribution they make toward the success of treatments. This is the heart of what Nelson and Hayes (1979a, 1979b) term "treatment validity," which has become their main concern (Hayes et al., 1986, 1987; Nelson, 1988).

In behavioral assessment, the situation is then very confusing. What seemed a frank and unanimous approach toward psychometric assessment is now being seriously debated. The coexistence of both movements in increasing disharmony creates almost "schizophrenic" situations (e.g., the appearance side by side of chapters such as those by Barrios and Hartmann and by Hayes et al. in the *Conceptual Foundations* of 1986, or of the chapters by Barrios and by Cone in Bellack & Hersen, 1988). It is because of this, as I mentioned in the introduction to this volume, that this subject must be treated with care. Numerous concepts and explanations related to psychometric standards have come out thus far; I will not be able to discuss each extensively here. For example, I shall hardly touch upon the issue of causality, otherwise so important, that is Nelson's third area of dissent. I have already said that I will focus, as closely as possible, on psychometric standards, touching upon related areas when they are clearly unavoidable. Perhaps the most important of these is idiographic interpretation, the topic of the next chapter.

Conclusion

Opinions gathered in the general framework of psychological assessment, as well as a movement within behavioral assessment evident over the past few years, presaged a sensitive approach of this discipline to psychometrics. What was at first brought up in relation to the weakness of psychometric improvement in behavioral instruments and its corresponding dangers has slowly led to a greater metric dependence on and sophistication in this instrumentation.

A small yet influential group of authors, including J. D. Cone and R. O. Nelson, however, rejects psychometric standards. In the eyes of these researchers, the behavioral model and the psychometric approach differ in three basic respects: the assumptions about behavior (psychometric assumptions of consistency and stability not being shared by the behavioral outlook), the level of analysis (group versus individual), and the model of causality (intrasubject structural causality versus setting-subject functional causality).

Thus current behavioral assessment is profoundly split with regard to the possibility of taking on psychometric standards. This makes it necessary that the question be reviewed in more detail and depth. First, in the next chapter I address the application and function of the idiographic approach in behavioral assessment. Once the manner in which behavioral assessment incorporates this term is explained, the primary problems will impinge on the relationship between idiographic and nomothetic approaches. In behavioral assessment a tendency emerges, although minor, to exclude completely the nomothetic approach, which is then viewed not only as far from the theoretical or methodological base of behavioral orientation but as actually unsound.

Second, and closely related to the first, some see the possibility of a normative interpretation of behavioral data, including a psychological differential focus that would complement the original focus that was centered on $N = 1$ (the study of intraindividual behavior variations in longitudinal designs). However, several authors have opposed a normative focus. I shall conclude that such a focus is not only convenient but necessary.

I shall later address the issue of reliability. The classic conception of reliability was tied to theoretical assumptions about behavior, particularly assumptions of consistency and stability. This has seemed to warrant rejection of this psychometric standard. Nevertheless, behavioral investigators have been less attentive to recent developments with respect to reliability that tend to relax the classical assumptions while maintaining a nucleus that seems indisputable. Alternative concepts that some behavioral assessors have proposed to substitute reliability in its psychometric sense—such as the concept of accuracy—face such serious problems that it is advisable to discard or at least completely revise them.

The topic of validity, which I will address afterwards, requires care. I will begin by clarifying the present psychometric concept of validity; there have been important advances beyond traditional notions. These advances will be seen in more detail in the chapters that develop criterion-related validity, content validity, and construct validity. Only in the light of these most recent developments can we review the relation between behavioral assessment and validity in its psychometric sense.

After clarifying the place of criterion-related validity in behavioral assessment—arguments by behavioral assessors that it has no place will be opportunely refuted—I will turn to content validity. In psychometric thought, this concept is en route to being merged into a single concept of validity, one that subordinates content validity to construct validity (as is also happening with criterion-related validity). This means that the debate about the relevance of validity in behavioral assessment must focus on construct validity. It is precisely with regard to constructs and construct validation that the harshest criticisms by some behavioral assessors have been made. For them, using constructs would be unnecessary and even pernicious. If constructs are avoided, construct validity is not a concern.

My detailed review of the concepts of *construct* and *construct validity* leads me to conclude that both are necessary to behavioral assessment. Behavioral assessment cannot disregard mediators and structurers of knowledge. Moreover, the process of behavioral assessment and, above all, the functional analysis that is its base should follow each of the phases of construct validation. These phases correspond to the construction, statement, and testing of scientific hypotheses.

Finally, Chapter 10 reviews, in some detail, the concept of *treatment validity*, which brings back the psychometric concept of utility that has been used since some pioneer projects in the 1950s. The recently renamed concept of *treatment utility* is important in the present and future perspectives of behavioral assessment as such, but some developments from it are defective and dangerous. I shall close with a final call for the integration of psychometric standards into behavioral assessment and of behavioral assessment into psychological assessment.

Notes

1. For a good summary of the pros and cons of the use of statistical tests in behavioral assessment, see Haynes (1983, 1991).

2. "Behavioral measures can and should be evaluated by the traditional psychometric criteria, and also by their utility, cost and effectiveness when the assessor provides data that will influence others' decisions" (Evans & Wilson, 1983, p. 47).

3. "The clinical utility of the behavioral approach is a function of the same factors (e.g., reliability, validity, reactivity, standardization, and the establishment of norms) with which traditional approaches have been contending for years. Therefore, it appears that behavioral assessors can certainly benefit by attending to the successes and failures of the traditional approach to assessment. Even though the two approaches are quite different, ignoring what has been accomplished in the past can only delay the further development of behavioral assessment" (Ciminero, 1986, p. 10).

4. "What we are arguing for is the recognition and acceptance of the conceptual issues, paradigms, and methodologies that transcend all approaches to assessment. These are conceptual issues, paradigms, and methodologies that must be attended to if any approach to assessment is to survive. To date, behavior therapists have paid little attention to these issues, paradigms, and methodologies, whereas students of traditional testing have been most mindful of them and, indeed, have attempted to design and evaluate their measurement practices in light of these preeminent concepts. The traditional approach to assessment is,

therefore, quite germane to the behavioral approach to assessment, in that it illustrates for us how these preeminent concepts guide us in the development and evaluation of our measurement practices" (Barrios & Hartmann, 1986, p. 82). "At each and every stage of assessment, there is some traditional notion or methodology that is relevant, if not necessary. And at each and every stage, the contribution is essentially the same, that of rendering more systematic and tenable the inferences that can be drawn from assessment data" (p. 105).

5. "This application of psychometrically evaluated assessment instruments within controlled settings and appropriate research designs can provide a strong test of the validity of clinical hypotheses and the efficacy of intervention (Bellack and Hersen, 1984)" (Haynes, 1990, p. 429). "Inferences derived from the application of inadequately developed or evaluated assessment must be viewed with extreme caution because the validity of the obtained measures [is] questionable. . . . [A] psychometric approach is necessary if behavioral assessment methods are to gain in acceptance and utility and their results are to be accurately and confidently interpreted" (Haynes, 1991, pp. 440, 451).

3

SOME OBSERVATIONS
ON THE IDIOGRAPHIC
APPROACH

Our point of departure for a more detailed review of the problematic issues noted throughout the preceding chapter, particularly with regard to criticisms by Cone and Nelson et al., is focused on the study of the *level of analysis*. This is the second area of divergence in Hayes et al. (1986), to the extent that here they face a group level (analysis made at the level of groups of people) and an individual level (the study of single cases).

It is known that behavioral assessors are, in general, advocates of the latter. They take a definite position regarding the old controversy between "extensive" and "intensive" designs (Chassan, 1960, 1979). The argument against the application of results obtained from group designs to the treatment of individual cases is nothing new in the experimental branch of assessment. Consider, for example, the work of Shapiro (1961a, 1961b). Summarized criticisms of the group perspective can also be found in

Hersen and Barlow (1976, 1984). Methodology specialists support these statements by pointing out that studies of single cases and studies of groups (or of "aggregates," in the terminology of Westmeyer) possess certain structures, logics, and aims that suggest that their results must be interpreted in different ways, and that they are, therefore, not interchangeable (Johnston & Pennypacker, 1980; Lamiell, 1987; Westmeyer, 1979). Hence the application field for single-case designs is not a leftover to be used only where group designs are not feasible. On the contrary, "the analyses of unique cases are the election method for testing all those hypotheses which pertain directly to statements about single individuals and not about aggregates of persons or . . . statistical averages of fictitious people" (Westmeyer, 1979, p. 21).

Although this thesis seems logically correct, many authors judge it to be bad advice. Knowledge of probabilistic population data may constitute a good heuristic in the analysis process and it is, above all, a mistake not to recognize such data in decision-making strategies. Across many individual cases, the picture from the reference group will naturally tend to repeat. Data from a group tell us nothing conclusive about any individual. Agreed—but they give clues for exploration and information to be considered when making decisions. It is for this reason that the cliché "We are not dealing with groups, we are dealing with this individual case" constitutes—in the words of Meehl (1973b)—a "vulgar error." The effort, very alive for certain investigators, to come up with special analysis designs that give information of interest regarding both the group and particular individuals should also not be forgotten (e.g., Epstein, 1983).

Let us focus on the role that idiographic interpretation plays in behavioral assessment. In the suggestions by Hayes et al. (1986) regarding level of analysis, there is much more than has been previously pointed out. There is the intention or, better yet, the requirement of identifying behavioral assessment with an idiographic focus of assessment. Cone (1986) summarizes the state of things well: "Perhaps nowhere else in psychology is Allport's idiographic perspective more relevant than in the newly emerged subdiscipline of behavioral assessment" (p. 111).

The idiographic emphasis appears in many of the already numerous "comparative tables" on traditional versus behavioral assessment (in the past decade or so, see, for instance, Barrios & Hartmann, 1986; or Fernández-Ballesteros, 1981a). It is repeated by authors such as Mischel (1968; with an affirmation as forceful as that recently cited by Cone), Schulte (1976), Haynes and Wilson (1979), and Wolpe (1986). Wolpe and Turkat (1985) infer from it that standardized procedures of assessment have limited importance. Naturally, the list of names could be considerably longer, but it is necessary to stop and reflect what this idiographic orientation has brought to behavioral assessment.

First, there is the concept of the *idiographic approach*. It is known that we are facing a prickly question that goes back to the beginning of the century and before, and to disciplines quite different from those that concern us today. This is not the place to review that development in detail; here I need only disentangle what behavioral assessors have said or meant to say. Both Goldfried (1981) and Mash (1985) point out that idiographic analysis has often been confused with "idiosyncratic" analysis, a confusion that has very few advantages and that makes the progress of the discipline much more difficult.

Not many behavioral assessors have made an effort to define what they understand by *idiographic,* perhaps because most think the term sufficiently clear (which is far from the truth). A first attempt at definition comes from Fernández-Ballesteros (1981a), who says that whereas traditional assessment typically functions with preestablished batteries, behavioral assessment "*is programmed for each case* (and, in this sense, we have qualified it as idiographic), because the particularities of each case make it necessary to use specific devices of measurement and/or assessment" (p. 82; see also Mischel, 1968; Peterson, 1968).

The idea is surely related to Shapiro's (1985) insistent proposal to take the relevant assessment variables from the problems of the individual—not using variables imposed "from outside"—thereby creating a highly individualized assessment design (e.g., Shapiro, 1961a, 1961b, 1964, 1970). It appears in even more detail in Mischel's works (he being understandably influenced by his mentor, George Kelly). One of his statements, at least, is worth quoting extensively:

My aim in writing *Personality and Assessment* was to defend individuality and the uniqueness of each person against the tendency (prevalent in clinical and diagnostic efforts in the 1960s) to use a few behavioral signs to categorize people enduringly into fixed slots on the assessor's favorite nomothetic trait dimensions. . . . Much of the assessor's task, it seemed to me, should be to help people in the search for such referents for their own personal constructs, instead of forcing the assessor's favorite dispositional labels on them. In our roles as clinicians, rather than leading clients to repackage their problems in our terms, with our constructs, we need to help them objectify *their* constructs into operational terms, so that they can achieve their own aims through more judicious arrangements of the conditions in their lives. We needed, I argued in *Personality and Assessment* (1968), to recognize the idiographic nature of each person while searching for the nomothetic principles, the general rules, that underlie behavior. . . . In the search for consistency, personologists emphasize their commitment to a focus on individuality (e.g., Carlson, 1971). Such a commitment requires serious recognition of the within-person patterning of attributes and behavior—the crux of the idiographic approach and the uniqueness of the person (e.g., Allport, 1937). (Mischel, 1984b, pp. 279-280, 290)

Let us return now to Cone and Nelson. Cone states that the idiographic investigation is "person centered," in the sense of focusing on the person's own characteristics. In such an investigation, the discovery of variables in a unique pattern is emphasized for each individual. Such relationships are examined intensively in order to record the variation in the subject through time. The individual's biography and the individual's own variables, rather than imposed variables or general and preestablished categories, are the points of departure. Therefore, the selection of the item content and of its grouping should be inductive (remember Shapiro's "personal question-naires"), and also the targets of intervention. Thus "the purest form of idiography might be one that studied behavior inductively as it varied over time within individuals" (Cone, 1986, p. 124). In any case, Cone insists that tones and degrees fit, and that we need to take other aspects into account (such as the longitudinal analysis of data) in order to account for the idiographic point of view in its concrete procedure. In short, Cone (1988) insists on the concept as well as the convenience of the idiographic approach, within what he calls the "idiographic-behavioral approach," described in Chapter 1.

The demand for an idiographic focus is also clearly present in the work of Nelson and her collaborators. In 1983, Nelson wrote that "for each client, an assessment process must be delineated that takes into account his or her unique problematic situations and response systems. For each client, target behaviors must be identified, treatment strategies selected, and outcome measures determined" (1983a, p. 201; see also Nelson, 1983b; Nelson & Hayes, 1986b). Likewise, intraindividual longitudinal designs are emphasized (Hayes et al., 1986).

To summarize, in the words of the behavioral assessors, an idiographic approach develops in the assessment of single cases (Plessen, 1981), and more concretely, not in the broad sense that Dukes (1965), for example, uses the formula $N = 1$, but rather in the sense of experimental longitudinal designs along the line of Campbell and Stanley (1963). The idiographic approach is simultaneously defined by three points:

1. The assessment process and its corresponding instrumentation are designed or chosen for each case. It is a "tailor-made" assessment.
2. The variables studied arise from the person and his or her environment; they are not imposed from outside. The perception of the subject being evaluated is seriously taken into account.

3. Assessment deals with the discovery and exploration of the pattern of variables (in this case, the behavioral pattern) that is typical of each person and unique to him or her.

As a matter of fact, it is on these three points—although at times not only these three and not with equal emphasis—that the majority of investigators have touched when proposing to characterize the idiographic approach. These points also correspond to the original formulations of Allport (e.g., 1937, 1962), which in turn move away from Stern's previous statements (Grossmann, 1986). Recent reviews on this subject likewise hit upon the points mentioned (Pervin, 1984; Runyan, 1983).

Such moderate statements about idiographic interpretation seem adequate; they speak neither of ineffable uniqueness nor of "holistic" foci that are nothing but utopian. It is, however, important to keep in mind the complexity contained in the study of individual patterns of variables—which, for example, forced Cone to use correlational and group designs repeatedly, as is the case in the multicontent-multimethod-multibehavior matrices (Cone, 1976) or in the "template matching" technique cited earlier (Cone & Hoier, 1986). It should also be remembered that the utility of the study of such patterns is still unproven, above all if it assumes moderator or configurational effects. In closely related fields of investigation simpler and more linear strategies of analysis have proven more powerful (e.g., Silva, 1988).

Idiographic Versus Nomothetic?

The most serious problems arise when idiographic statements—in themselves correct—give rise to some derivations. At least with Nelson (1983a; Hayes et al., 1986) such statements are accompanied by a rejection of psychometric principles and subsequently of psychometric standards of quality. Fernández-Ballesteros (1984) fittingly replies that idiographic interpretation does not imply disregard of reliability and validity. Strosahl and Linehan (1986) observe that explanations such as Nelson's are in danger of giving a vote of confidence to the precision, reliability, and validity of behavioral assessment procedures, which in light of a series of proven biases and of the still limited existing investigation of them seems, at least, a little premature. To propose, as Nelson (1981) does, the development of an "idiographic psychometry" (which is nothing new; consider the examples given by Chassan, 1960; Huber, 1973; R. R. Jones, 1973) is without a doubt an interesting idea, but it does not resolve the problem of quality standards.

Another fundamental issue is the relation between the idiographic and the nomothetic. I must first clarify that the authors cited above indiscriminately use the term *nomothetic* to refer to group or interindividual difference studies, and to refer to general (or at least supraindividual) laws. I have already noted that Cone, although he criticizes them, has had to use group designs. This is also true for Nelson et al. when it comes to selecting behavioral objectives (Nelson & Hayes, 1986b) or determining treatment validity (Hayes et al., 1986). Nelson does admit the collaboration of nomothetic information, although in a subordinate form. In 1981, she wrote:

> It has been a behavioral tradition to focus on the individual subject or client. An empirical clinical science, however, demands general principles which are universally applicable.
>
> Therefore, it seems advantageous to search in behavioral assessment for nomothetic or general principles which can then be utilized in an idiographic or individualized manner. . . . Identified nomothetic patterns often allow for a good deal of idiographic variability as well. (Nelson & Hayes, 1981, pp. 12-13)

Several years later, she broadened what she recognized as the field of action of nomothetic approaches in behavioral assessment. These approaches would be useful in (a) the use of normative data (to be addressed in the next chapter), (b) the use of general principles arising from abnormal psychology, and (c) the use of diagnostic labels in scientific communication.

The "general principles arising from abnormal psychology" may refer to frequent response covariations, variables that typically control an established behavior, or frequent success of a concrete treatment on a specific behavioral disorder. "Of course," Nelson remarks, "these general principles must be applied idiographically to the client in question" (Nelson & Hayes, 1986b, p. 10; see also Nelson, 1987). Indeed, and in spite of the above-cited texts, Nelson repeatedly seems to reject nomothetic approaches. She also proposes an "inductive clinical science" (Nelson, 1983a, p. 201)—that is, a science "whose general principles are derived from an analysis of individuals"—as a way of reaching nomothetic explanations.

To his polarizing of assessment models, Cone (1988) is much more emphatic in his rejection of the nomothetic. He too claims an inductive approach to generalization through a series of single-case studies (Cone, 1988)—although the meaning given the term *induction* is not always clear. This aspiration connects with the backbone of single-case experimental designs (e.g., Hersen & Barlow, 1976, 1984; Kratochwill, 1978; Sidman, 1960).

The majority of behavioral assessors, however, seem not to reject the nomothetic approach. Evans and Wilson (1983) point to the utopian nature and the impoverishment of this rejection; the latter is also mentioned by Strosahl and Linehan (1986). The idea is that the idiographic interpretation does not exclude nomothetics, but rather that we deal with two complementary perspectives that mutually enrich each other (Fernández-Ballesteros

1984; Kendall, 1984; Strosahl & Linehan, 1986) and that receive different importance depending on the stage of the assessment process (Bellack & Hersen, 1988).

The idiographic/nomothetic contrast is not particular to behavioral assessment; in reality it arises from the broader framework of psychological assessment and indeed from the methodology of social sciences in general. It would be wise to take a look at this broader framework.

Are foci incompatible? Does adopting one imply rejecting the other? Cronbach (1984a) reminds us that "Allport (1937), who gave the words their place in psychology, emphasized that the approaches are supplementary, not antagonistic" (p. 502; see also Allport, 1962; Marceil, 1977; Pervin, 1984; Tous, 1986). Allport's (1942) observation that the "general laws of human behavior known to us are altered and sometimes negated by the idiographic knowledge available to us concerning the personality we are studying" (p. 58) does nothing more than express the dialectic that occurs between knowledge of the specific and the general, between reality and concept, between data and law. This is found in all other sciences (Franck, 1986). Windelband stated that the idiographic approaches need nomothetics, in the sense that they need general laws (see Grossmann, 1986). Rickert, another of the more outstanding representatives of the idiographic approach, completely recognizes the need to use concepts even to make individual descriptions, as well as the need for a nomothetic focus in order to formulate such concepts (see Musso, 1970). We can go beyond this and find, for example, in Dilthey (1951)—an author who very directly influenced the birth of the idiographic movement—statements similar to this one of Eysenck (1971): "For a man of science, the single individual is simply the point of intersection of a certain number of quantitative variables" (p. 19). Musso (1970), who made a detailed study of the controversy between the idiographic and the nomothetic, states:

> There are no sciences which are concerned with the discovery of general laws that leave aside the study of individual cases, nor vice versa. . . . Hence, sciences are idiographic and nomothetic; not idiographic or nomothetic, as Windelband and Rickert believed. (pp. 276-277)

Writers on the psychology of personality, who clearly support the idiographic approach, see a necessary relation with the nomothetic (e.g., Bem, 1983; Pervin, 1984; Runyan, 1983). An attempt at synthesis is made by Harris (1980) and, above all, in a proposal of an "idiothetic" psychology of personality (Lamiell, 1981, 1982; Lamiell, Foss, Larsen, & Hempel, 1983; Lamiell & Trierweiler, 1986). Mischel had already clearly noted, in his 1968 book, that "although every individual, and indeed every response pattern, is in a sense unique, the basic processes that determine his behavior are not" (p. 188). Along this same line, Fernández-Ballesteros (1983b) suggests that synthesis of the idiographic and nomothetic is needed for psychodiagnostics:

> 1. The objectives of Psychodiagnostics are fundamentally idiographic in the sense that they focus on the scientific study of the behavior of a subject.
> 2. Psychodiagnostics is based on the findings of a nomothetic discipline and, due to this, on the laws established for multiple psychological facts. (p. 62; see also Fernández-Ballesteros, 1980)

Surely, the greater part of the misunderstanding that surfaces at times is not caused by opposition between individual facts and general laws, but rather by the way laws are reached. Some authors insist on the difficulties and even the inconsistencies that may arise from wanting to derive laws from group designs and to apply formulas obtained from group studies to individual cases. However, that strategy is not the only one possible for obtaining general formulations. There is an illustrious tradition in psychology (see Lewin, 1973) in which the formulation of general laws stems directly from the intensive study of individual cases. Many authors see no contradiction between the lawful and the individual. On the contrary, a law ought to be manifested in each and every individual. This tradition is shared by authors such as Pavlov, Thorndike, Watson, and Skinner, to name only a few of the great founders of modern behaviorism, which is, in turn, the matrix of behavior therapy and of behavioral assessment. Laws of learning were not derived from means and standard deviations of conglomerate data from many subjects. If we pay close attention, we will see that Allport protests, above all else, against a grouplike way of facing an individual case, but not against the lawfulness of the same. In this sense, Pervin (1984) points out that "utilization of the idiographic approach in no way runs counter to the pursuit of general laws. To the contrary, the idiographic method is seen as useful in the discovery of such laws" (p. 278).

To progress, we must remember that the central task of behavioral assessment, functional analysis, ends up proposing an explanatory model of target behaviors. This is bolstered by invoking laws of learning or, in broader terms, laws concerning the psychological processes entering the interaction between subject and environment. In other words, it has to do with proposing a theoretical model of behavior (Sundberg, 1977) by stating which "general principles established by psychology in its different specialties are given into this individual subject" (Fernández-Ballesteros, 1983b, pp. 47-48; see also Tous, 1989). Thus we cannot accept, as Hayes et al. (1986) would like, that in behavioral assessment "few theoretical assumptions are made about the nature and role of a given behavior" (p. 466). I shall return to this important point in Chapter 9, in the discussion of construct validity. It is interesting to note that the logical functioning of such process is essentially deductive or, better said, hypothetical-deductive. In the words of Westmeyer (1972), and consistent with the deterministic representation characteristic of behaviorist theories, the explanation of a particular behavior is "deductive-nomological," not "inductive-statistical" (whose explanatory power has been seriously questioned in the theory of science, as well as in psychology; see, e.g., Pulver, 1978b). The structure is as follows: From the lawlike formulations and from the conditions (*explanans* or antecedents) logically follows the *explanandum* (consequent). In terms of behavioral assessment, the lawlike formulations are the "laws of behavior" and the *explanandum,* the behavior in question. In this way, a complete assessment can be accomplished only when, on the basis of a specified behavioral principle, the conditions on which the problematic behavior depends are established (Dachener, 1981).

It is interesting to note the insistence with which both Cone (1981b, 1988; Cone & Hoier, 1986) and Nelson et al. (Hayes et al., 1986; Nelson & Hayes, 1986b) have recently claimed to be using an inductive approach. It is true that at times the term seems to take on a different sense (for example, in order to design the act of extracting the variables of interest directly from the subject, and not on the basis of preestablished dimensions). Yet the expression *inductive clinical science,* which Nelson repeats (1983a; see also Hayes et al., 1986; Nelson & Maser, 1988), is in no way ambiguous. This expression is along the line of the advancement in the generalization of results across direct and systematic replication designs. It must, however, be mentioned that such an approach to generalization—especially when it attempts to generalize from laboratory conditions as if they were natural conditions—has been placed under severe criticism (Westmeyer, 1979). On the other hand, there may be confusion between the discovery of principles or laws of behavior and empirical delimitation of their field of applicability. As a matter of fact, assessment has to do with the latter, because of its technological aspect, because assessment is more within the realm of *applying* a science and less within the realm of constructing one. The strategy of direct and systematic replications fits with the applied aspect. It does not deal with the eventual formulation of laws or principles, but rather with limiting its domain in practice. From a behavioral perspective, these remarks ought to be kept in mind before one speaks of an inductive clinical **science.**

Conclusions

This chapter begins a systematic review of the problematic topics listed in Chapter 2. The proposed difference in analysis level—group versus individual—focuses on the defense, common to almost all behavioral assessors, of an idiographic approach that fundamentally means (a) that the assessment process and its corresponding instrumentation are designed or chosen for each case ("tailor-made" assessment), (b) that the variables that are studied stem from the person and his or her environment, and (c) that an attempt is made to discover a unique structure of variables for each person.

These moderate statements of idiographic interpretation seem acceptable, even though some of them may encounter great practical difficulties and their utility is not wholly established. Broader problems arise when such statements are accompanied by rejection of any nomothetic approach. This represents a minority posture in behavioral assessment, although it is not to be ignored. This chapter has demonstrated the unsoundness of that rejection, above all when one is proposing functional hypotheses that are based on learning processes within general reach.

To the extent that some behavioral assessors mix two aspects of nomothetics, nomothetic as reference to group studies and nomothetic as reference to general laws, a frequent confusion is produced with regard to the inductive or deductive character of behavioral assessment. It is appropriate here to emphasize that behavioral psychology has typically worked—in accordance with traditions of psychological science that go back to Weber and Fechner—with studies of single subjects from which hypotheses have been directly drawn about the laws of behavior. Yet, in the applied work of behavioral assessment, the road followed when postulating and contrasting working hypotheses is inverse and essentially deductive. Depending on knowledge of psychological processes, mainly learning processes, we attempt to discover which ones best explain the behavior in question. Some authors speak of an *inductive clinical science* that derives its general principles from the analysis of many individuals by means of replication designs, but these remarks seem to confuse construction and application of science. To insist on the intended meaning of the expression *inductive clinical science* would result in a frankly unorthodox deviation from the bases of behavioral science.

4

BEHAVIORAL ASSESSMENT AND NORMATIVE INTERPRETATION

Related to the question of "group versus individual perspective" and, more directly, to the importance given to interindividual versus intraindividual differences is the consideration of normative scores in behavioral assessment. It is known that, in light of the dominant tendency for normative interpretation of test scores, Glaser, in the framework of educational assessment, proposed the alternative of basing an interpretation on "criteria." He also created the basis for a criterion technology of test construction. A *criterion-referenced test* is one interpreted with regard to "absolute quality status," whereas a *norm-referenced test* is interpreted based on standing relative to a group (Glaser, 1963). Thus "a criterion-referenced test is one that is deliberately constructed to yield measurements that are directly interpretable in terms of specified performance standards" (Glaser & Nitko, 1971, p. 653).

The terminology *criterion-oriented test* or *criterion-referenced test* was readily accepted by the scientific community and spread quickly. It continues to be used—in behavioral assessment, among other fields—in spite of the suggestion of the American Psychological Association that the name be changed in order to avoid the use of the word *criterion,* which has two different meanings: In psychological assessment that term has traditionally been used to designate the variable to be predicted, and correspondingly with reference to "criterion-related validity." Use of *content-referenced* (American Psychological Association [APA], American Educational Research Association [AERA], & National Council on Measurement in Education [NCME], 1974) or *domain-referenced* (AERA, APA, & NCME, 1985; Anastasi, 1988; Cronbach, 1984a) has been proposed. According to the *Standards* of 1974:

> Interpretations of test scores traditionally have been *norm-referenced*; that is, an individual's score is interpreted in terms of comparisons with scores made by other individuals. Alternative interpretations are possible. *Content-referenced* interpretations are those where the score is directly interpreted in terms of performance at each point of the achievement continuum being measured. *Criterion-referenced* interpretations are those where the score is directly interpreted in terms of performance at any given point on the continuum of an *external* variable. (APA, AERA, & NCME, 1974, p. 19)

For Cronbach (1984a):

> A *norm-referenced* report tells where the person stands among others who took the test. A *domain-referenced* report tells at what level of difficulty a person can cope with a specified kind of task. . . . A *criterion-referenced* report views the score as a sign that the person can or cannot be expected to satisfy some practically significant requirement. (p. 87)

After the continued dual use (e.g., Anastasi, 1988; Nunnally, 1978) of the term *criterion,* the definitions of *domain-referenced tests* and *criterion-referenced tests* have tended toward assimilation (Messick, 1989). Interpretation is made for a specified domain of content or for a level of performance, without regard to the performance of other people (AERA, APA, & NCME, 1985).

Glaser's suggestion for interpretation of scores in the educational field was favorably accepted in psychological assessment. It is not my aim to review this approach in detail; some points will suffice. Carver (1974) proposed a distinction between two dimensions of tests: a psychometric dimension that focuses on the measurement of stable interindividual differences and an edumetric dimension that focuses on the measurement of intraindividual changes. As Glaser insisted upon and other authors have detailed (e.g., Popham, 1978), the judgment on the metric quality of an instrument depends on which perspective is taken. It was at a meeting of German-speaking psychologists, which was monographically dedicated to assessment (Pulver, Lang, & Schmid, 1978), that Pulver (1978a) insisted that the restriction psychodiagnostics was suffering from was mainly due to its concentration on diagnostics based on standardized instrumentation and normative interpretations. He also suggested that a singular focus on instruments ought to be fostered in order to make hypotheses on particular modes of functioning (Pulver, 1978b). This point of view was also well received in Eastern Europe (Schaarschmidt, 1984). The nonnormative focus is precisely what inspired Lamiell to advocate an "idiothetic" perspective in personality assessment. Lamiell's explanation falls into the framework of intraindividual differences (e.g., Lamiell & Trierweiler, 1986), namely, between what an individual in fact achieves and what he or she does not but *could* achieve. Thus the relationship between this approach and that of "learning potential" is clear.

Indeed, the norm-referenced/criterion-referenced distinction has been resolutely adopted by behavioral assessment. In tables that compare traditional assessment with behavioral assessment, reference to norms is typically placed in the former and reference to criteria in the latter. This appears, for example, in Pawlik's (1976) list of the four most important differences distinguishing a traditional from a behavioral approach to diagnostics. He adds that the distinction must not overlook prediction nor assume that a criterion-oriented focus will take away importance from interindividual differences, because exactly the opposite occurs. Fernández-Ballesteros (1979) also mentions a relation between a criterion-referenced focus and behavioral assessment, and between norm-referenced and traditional assessment. Linehan (1980) touches on this same point and attempts to define the criterion-referenced tests in the same manner as above. She takes Livingston's (1977) observations on the importance of content validity in the criterion approach and attempts to pinpoint the parallel between criterion-referenced tests and behavioral assessment. The final aspects are developed in detail in the complete comparison made by Martínez Arias (1981) between educational and behavioral assessment, on the one hand, and traditional psychological assessment, on the other. The latter two authors insist on the absolute meaning of criterion-oriented scores as opposed to the relative or derived meaning of normative scores. Plessen (1981) is interested in emphasizing the importance of the criterion-referenced approach for an assessment that, like the behavioral one, is essentially directed toward therapeutic goals:

This diagnostic approach makes it possible to establish how close a client has gotten to a determined criterion—in this case the therapeutic goal, independent of the levels reached by the other clients with regard to that criterion. For this reason, the therapeutic goal-oriented diagnosis must be distinguished from the traditional diagnosis oriented toward norms. While the traditional diagnosis provides information about the position of the subject with regard to the average of its reference population, thus operating with real norms, in the diagnosis oriented toward criteria, ideal norms are applied. The ideal norms refer to a determined *a priori* state (in this case, the therapeutic goal) which must be redefined for each individual even though it may possess some general validity. Measurements oriented toward therapeutic goals compare the state of the client with the predetermined criterion. For that reason, the ideal norm and the criterion standard are identical. (p. 73; see also the 1986 personal communication from S. W. Bijou cited in Carbonell, 1987)

Are Criterions and Norms Referenced Measurements Incompatible?

The author who has most insistently defended the application of the criterion-referenced as opposed to the norm-referenced approach in behavioral assessment is Cone. Cone and Hawkins (1977a) recognized the auxiliary role that norms may play in guiding the study of criteria or even in setting them up. However, they conclude that "norms will no longer be the exclusive reference points for interpreting individual scores as they have been in the past" (pp. 389-390). This statement contains (probably unintentionally) a serious error: In psychological assessment, norms have never been the only point of reference for interpreting individual scores. The most important points of reference are in validation studies, in turn modulated by a series of considerations. Cone (1978b) returned to the matter a year later and, extensively, in 1981:

> Whatever dimensional quantity we select to observe, the significance we attach to the values obtained derives from comparing them with some relatively absolute standard of effective performance. In this regard, behavioral assessment is criterion-referenced (Livingston, 1977). This perspective is in sharp contrast to the traditional practice of assigning significance to scores based on comparison with the average or normal performance of a group of persons. (Cone, 1981b, p. 54)

The idea is also present in Cone's (1986, 1988) attempt to differentiate types of behavioral assessment. In short, "normism" is denounced as an unorthodox tendency in this discipline. Although some utility is recognized in norms, "it is unlikely that norms would ever be the most appropriate reference points for selecting intervention targets and judging the effectiveness or social validity of intervention efforts in the single case" (Cone & Hoier, 1986).

This radical rejection of the normative approach is the exception rather than the rule among behavioral assessors. It is interesting to recall that Weiss (1968), in one of the first works on behavioral assessment, succeeded in making it clear that an operant approach is perfectly compatible with an individual differences perspective. Weiss felt that the foci complement and mutually enrich each other. Allow this remark to serve as a general frame of reference. Returning to the specific question of the utility of norms, it is also interesting to note that Dickson (1975), clearly in favor of an experimental paradigm of assessment and suspicious of standardization of procedures, strongly claims the usefulness of norms:

> The need for norms within the functional analysis approach cannot be stressed too much. What are the acceptable standards for behaviors within today's society? What constitutes aggressive acting-out behavior within a particular classroom? What frequency of communication can be labeled a behavioral deficit? The logical extension of the Kanfer-Saslow (1969) model of behavioral analysis is the establishment of norms for particular environments. Before a functional analysis can have meaning, the behavior in question must be related to client baselines, situational expectations, and peer performances. Only after this information is gathered should intervention take place. (p. 379)

Two years later, in the first systematic explanation of "social validity" as a standard to be considered at different times during behavior assessment and therapy, Kazdin (1977b; see also Wolf, 1978) repeatedly reverts to the normative perspective. One of the two general procedures Kazdin proposed in order to achieve an estimation of social validity is comparison of the client with peers who are not identified as having problems with respect to the target behavior. According to Kazdin, normative data are required to aid in both the identification of clients and the evaluation of treatment effects. Normative data, by adding objectivity and precision, also complement the second aspect of social validity: subjective evaluation. Therefore, Kazdin (1977b) suggests fostering normative studies, as well as research on the variables that moderate the application and interpretation of norms: "Normative data and subjective evaluation seem to be essential additions to overt behavioral data" (p. 448). Certainly, the requirement of social validity has been criticized (Deitz, 1978; Fuqua & Schwade, 1986), but not for its normative perspective. On the contrary, its weak points are in part reduced by serious consideration of normative-type data (Fuqua & Schwade, 1986; see also Barrios & Hartmann, 1986).

The requirement for a normative focus continues. Hartmann et al. (1979) bring up the persistent problem of the ambiguous meaning of scores, including problems related to behavioral assessment instruments (see also Evans & Nelson, 1977; Goldfried, 1981; Schaller & Schmidtke, 1983). Kanfer and Nay (1982) point out that the normative approach has been too narrowly interpreted. In fact, it is present during the use of any type of instrument, and in the form of implicit or explicit judgments made by the practitioner throughout the assessment process. For instance, it is seen in the knowledge of base rates and of cultural norms in which the behavior of a client develops. Its disregard could lead to serious errors of interpretation. Thus, "we believe that the development of interindividual norms to complement the intraindividual, criterion-referenced approach . . . is badly needed for many of the decisions that assessors must make" (Kanfer & Nay, 1982, p. 377; see also Haynes, 1990, 1991).

Both Kratochwill (1985) and Kendall (1984, 1985) examine this point in retrospect, finding a series of uses for normative data regarding multiple problems and populations. We should also remember that normative assessment stands out in dealing with children and youth, where developmental norms must be taken into account. Barrios and Hartmann (1986) remind us that the criterion to which we must pay attention when considering whether a behavior is appropriate or inappropriate is not always clear. Fixing such a criterion may lead to too rigid a posture. In the face of such issues, a normative approach is useful, and so supports its utility in the phases of identification of problematic behavior, as well as in the appraisal of therapeutic outcomes. Nelson and Hayes (1986b) emphasize this, making the utility of a normative approach clear when it comes to using empirical keys to select behavioral targets.

On the other hand, in the broader framework of psychometric assessment there have been cautions concerning criterion-referenced interpretation. It is not that the legitimacy of this type of interpretation, or its utility for dealing with intraindividual approaches or those oriented toward the assessment of change, is in question. What is in question is whether or not it is completely different from and independent of a normative approach. For example, Messick (1975) states that all procedures for establishing standards of achievement require expert appraisal that often contains normative comparisons, explicit or implicit. In their review of test theory and methods, Weiss and Davison (1981) note that normative information comes into the establishment of criteria, "a practice which blurs the distinction between norm and criterion-referenced testing but which helps avoid unrealistically high or low criteria" (pp. 635-636). Other authors have made similar remarks. Thus Anastasi (1988) underlines that "such an interpretation [criterion-referenced] can certainly be combined with norm-referenced scores" (p. 103). "It should be noted that criterion-referenced testing is neither as new nor as clearly divorced from norm-referenced testing as some of its proponents implied" (p. 105).

The underlying question is whether it is possible to fix criteria for the behavior of a certain subject without using the behavior of others as a frame of reference, perhaps implicit. Epstein (1983), among others, denies this possibility. Lamiell and Trierweiler (1986) reply that a normative approach is preceded by a nonnormative one, to the extent that for a normative approach to be effective, it needs instruments—and these mark the limits for any norm that may later be constructed. These authors call this "a frame of reference that is fundamentally non-normative" (p. 480; see also Lamiell, 1987). But this interpretation is questionable. It is difficult to think that a test may be conceived—let alone produced—without more or less explicit reference to the population to which it will be applied. A test is obviously preliminary to norms that may be obtained from it, but not to the normative frame the test creator has in mind if he or she wants the test to reflect reality. Because of this, I cannot but agree with Anastasi's (1988) remark that "a normative framework is implicit in all testing, regardless of how scores are expressed (Angoff, 1974; Nitko, 1984)" (p. 106).

Conclusion

The general conclusion that can be reached from this chapter is similar to that reached in the previous chapter: The dual foci—the idiographic and the nomothetic, the interindividual and the intraindividual—must not be seen as opposed or exclusive; they converge and complement each other. Barrios and Hartmann (1986) state that "data, even behavioral assessment data, have no intrinsic meaning. It is when assessment data are interpreted—set against the yardstick of normative and/or generalizability estimates—that they acquire significance (Kaplan, 1964; Mitroff & Sagasti, 1973)" (p. 98). Barrios (1988) presents an appropriate synthesis of the topic of norms:

> Traditionally, therapists have shied away from making . . . interindividual comparisons, for they believe that group data were not particularly pertinent to the individual case (e.g., Barlow and Hersen, 1984; Hartmann et al., 1979; Nelson and Hayes, 1979[a]). As a consequence, there are few assessment devices for which we have norms for various reference groups (Barrios and Shigetomi, 1985; Evans and Nelson, 1977). Thus, we have a few occasions on which to use a norm-referenced approach to data interpretation. Lately, we have come to look more kindly toward group data and have come to temper the belief that group data are irrelevant to the individual case. This turnaround in therapists' attitudes toward group data is due largely to an increased awareness and appreciation of the role that norms can play in the

practice and progress of behavior therapy (Barrios & Hartmann, 1986; Hartmann et al., 1979). Norms can be of great help in screening prospective clients, identifying performance deficits, defining problematic behaviors, determining treatment targets, designing powerful treatments, selecting optimum treatments, establishing treatment goals, forming homogeneous groups, describing client samples, comparing alternative measures, and gauging treatment outcomes (e.g., Cone & Hawkins, 1977[a]; Evans & Nelson, 1977; Hartmann et al., 1979; Kazdin, 1977[a]; Wolf, 1978). Of course, norms are of no help in carrying out any of these therapeutic functions if there are no normative estimates for the instruments employed and for the clients with whom they are employed. This is, in fact, the situation for most of the instruments used with the majority of clients. It may, however, be a situation that is changing. For with the changing view toward group data, we are seeing more collection of normative data (e.g., McGlynn et al., 1987; Ollendick, 1983). We are thus seeing the creation of more opportunities for the use of a normreferenced approach to data interpretation. (pp. 28-29)

The above review of the norm/criterion question has led us to relativize the alleged absolute value of the latter. It is now time to enter into the field of generalizability. With that we will take a step forward in our review of the main psychometric standards in behavioral assessment.

5

THE PROBLEM OF
RELIABILITY

If we disregard some minor differences, it may be said that there is a broad consensus among behavioral assessors with regard to the psychometric standard known as reliability. In a word, the focal assumptions about behavior are criticized. They are well explained and summarized in the previously cited text by Hayes et al. (1986) in reference to differences between behavioral and psychometric approaches. Behavioral assessors reject the interpretation of the observed score as consisting of true value plus measurement error, or, more concretely, they reject the interpretation of that "true" value as something consistent and stable. Taking consistency and stability as criteria of score quality implies an assumption that behavior is consistent and stable—an assumption made in trait theory. In the behavioral approach there exists, however, a long critical tradition with regard to the alleged consistency and stability of behavior. Recall, among others, Mischel's (1968) *Personality and Assessment.*

A behavioral approach does not imply an "assumption" of inconsistency and instability, as some have wanted to see it. Rather, it implies considering observed consistency or inconsistency, stability or instability, as empirical facts requiring explanation. Inconsistency or instability in scores may well reflect inconsistent or unstable behavior. Hence it is wrong to consider a measurement a priori deficient in quality if high indexes of consistency and stability are not attained. Nelson et al. said this in 1977, criticizing Cone's (1977b) early thoughts on reliability and validity in behavioral assessment. Cone himself later took this critical position (Cone, 1978b, 1981b, 1986, 1987a, 1988; see also Barrios & Hartmann, 1986; Nelson, 1983b; Silva, 1978).

However, criticisms of the traditional interpretation of reliability had long been evident in the psychometric literature. I will cover only a few aspects here. Among criticisms made of the traditional interpretation of reliability are those discussed below.

First, the alleged random behavior of error variance has been looked at with suspicion (e.g., Hoermann, 1964). That view should be replaced by a more refined one in which both systematic and nonsystematic measurement errors are considered. Also, random assumption characteristic of behavior ought to be distinguished from an assumption about a random distribution of measurement error. Behavioral psychologists—and many others—are right to insist that there is no random behavior. Accepting that does not make it necessary to deny that error variance is random. On the contrary, if it were thought that chance enters into assessed behavior, then random effects would be included in true variance and not in error variance. It is one thing to suggest that chance has no place in the theory of behavior and quite another to say that "'error' has no place in behavioral theory" (Hayes et al., 1986, p. 472). Such a statement confuses behavior and measurement of behavior and risks granting a character of perfection to measurement. Strosahl and Linehan (1986) have already been quoted on this danger; let me also quote Anastasi (1988): "Any single observation, however obtained, contains an error of measurement; ignoring this error will not make it go away" (p. 510; see also Suen & Ary, 1989).

Second, however much some psychometric theoreticians insist that the concept of true value must be understood in a methodological sense and not a metaphysical one, it is difficult not to see in it what May (1955) calls "hunger for reality." March (1957) detects a realist thought underlying that concept. Hoermann (1964) speaks of naive realism and others of a platonic approach (e.g., Lumsden, 1976). Although the concept of universe score has similarities to that of true score, the theory of generalizability within which it is framed does seem to contribute in this matter. I shall return to this point further on.

The assumptions of consistency and stability have also been criticized within the psychometric tradition. For example, Tallent (1965), following ideas of Symonds, points out that "a test which accurately mirrors personality should show low or moderate test-retest reliability with respect to those aspects of behavior which are expected to be changeable" (p. 431; see also Byrne, 1964; Levy, 1973). Raven (1966) captures this same idea:

> A psychologist may want a person's performance to be the same throughout a test, or he may want to record its variations as the test proceeds. In the former case a test with a high co-efficient of internal consistency will be desirable; in the latter case it will be undesirable. . . .
> Again a test may show a high or low test retest correlation co-efficient. As a result the test is said to be "reliable" or "unreliable," We have still to ask the question, 'reliable or unreliable for what?' All a test retest correlation co-efficient shows is the degree to which a psychologist can expect the same result when the test is repeated. If, during the time between the tests, a person's output of the activity measured by the test has changed, a high retest correlation only means that the test fails to record the change that has taken place. It is therefore a "good" test if we do not want to record this change, but a "bad" test if we do want to record it. In exactly the same way a test which gives a low retest correlation coefficient will be a "bad" test if this is because the results vary independently of the activity it is supposed to assess. It is, however, a "good" test if the results can be shown to be sensitive to variations in the activity assessed, provided, of course, that the psychologist wants to use the test to observe and record these variations. (pp. 54-55; see also Raven, 1989)[1]

Little can be added to these words, with which no behavioral assessor can disagree. Raven's ideas are not isolated within the psychometric development of the past few decades (e.g., Anastasi, 1988). It is interesting to review the evolution in the *Standards* of the APA, which constitute one of the primary expressions of quality standards for measurement in psychology. In 1954 and 1966, the concept of reliability was identified with consistency and stability: "Reliability refers to the accuracy (consistency and stability) of measurement by a test" (APA, 1966, p. 182). In 1974, the concept clearly returned to its origins, to defining reliability according to the degree of error in measurement: "Reliability refers to the degree to which the results of testing are attributable to systematic sources of variance" (APA, AERA, & NCME, 1974, p. 48). If terms such as *consistency* and *stability* continue to be used, it is not in the strict sense of internal consistency and temporal stability characteristic of a specific conception of behavior, but rather as the basic reproducibility of results fundamental to scientific research. Reliability is "the degree to which test scores are consistent, dependable, or repeatable, that is, the degree to which they are free of errors of measurement," as defined by the AERA, APA, and NCME (1985, p. 93). Johnston and Pennypacker (1980) state that "reliability is concerned with the stability of measured values under constant conditions" (p. 191). Consistency and stability of obtained scores are required if and only if there is nothing that suggests that what is assessed may have been modified.[2]

Contributions of the Theory of Generalizability

The most important step toward recovering reliability from the substantialist bases where classical authors had placed it is surely in the theory of generalizability, proposed by Cronbach et al. at the beginning of the 1960s (Cronbach et al., 1963) and, above all, in their book of 1972. This theory, which at first only alleged to "liberalize" the concept of reliability and its applications, has had profound impact on the theory of psychometric standards of quality, as we shall see later (e.g., Silva, 1982, 1984; Wiggins, 1973).

In behavioral assessment, the application of generalizability theory has proven controversial. Coates and Thoresen (1978), for example, favor its application, and attempt to answer strong criticisms by R. R. Jones (1977) with respect to longitudinal studies of single cases (Strossen, Coates, & Thoresen, 1979). Indeed, this is not the framework of individual differences in which generalizability theory (or reliability theory) developed (e.g., Cronbach, 1984a). Cone (1977b), who at one point attempted to use generalizability theory as the comprehensive framework for decomposing sources of observed score variance in behavioral assessment, abandoned it and later criticized it because he saw it as centered on individual differences (Cone, 1981b, 1987b). This line, one that Nelson et al. also follow, has already been covered sufficiently. However, clear paths to solve the problem related to the application of generalizability theory to $N = 1$ have recently appeared (e.g., Shavelson, Webb, & Rowley, 1989; Suen & Ary, 1989).

The value of the *theoretical* upset brought about by generalizability theory has not been emphasized in behavioral assessment (Coates & Thoresen, 1978). Authors tend to applaud the breakdown of score variance and the detection of the magnitude of different errors from specific sources. This methodological contribution is also the feature most emphasized in the psychometric tradition (see the *Standards* of 1974 and 1985). However, more fundamental is an epistemological reorientation, leading away from the realism associated with traditional reliability theory.

The traditional approach dealt with the true score as though it were transcendental, pertaining to the assessed object beyond all perspective. Now the claim is more humble: Is it possible to generalize? And more specifically, Through what concrete dimensions can I, or am I supposed to, generalize? The question of the true value turns then into a question of generalization from sample to universe, and "the question of 'reliability' thus resolves into a question of accuracy of generalization, or generalizability" (Cronbach et al., 1972, p. 15). A score is essentially relative to the perspective of generalization taken (people or conditions—observers, elements, time, situations) and from there one can speak not of true score but rather of "universe score":

> Any observation . . . fits within a variety of universes. "The universe score is estimated to be 75" is without meaning until we answer the question, "Which universe?" This ambiguity is concealed in the statement "The estimated true score is 75," for no one thinks to inquire, "Which truth?" (pp. 18-19)

In short, if we no longer deal with the search for a true score but rather with consideration of alternative universes of generalization, the question arises: In which of them should we move? The answer is pragmatic: It depends on the goal of assessment. In some cases, the interest will be placed on generalization across time, and this universe will move to the foreground; in other cases, the interest will be placed on generalization across situations, and so on. Cronbach (1957) pointed out that the traditional psychometric approach corresponds only to one conception of behavior and also to established problems and assessment tasks: those of selection and classification. With regard to such problems and tasks, it is clear that questions of consistency and temporal stability gain importance. However, a different perspective is possible (Cronbach, 1957; Pawlik, 1976). For that reason, those questions may be put aside in favor of a focus on more important ones. A dialectic between the conception of behavior and the action taken is brought up, for which generalizability theory is a sound approach.

There is, at least, one more substantial contribution. Upon converting the problem of reliability into a problem of generalization, Cronbach et al. constructed a conceptual bridge between reliability and validity that may become definitive. As a matter of fact, if the universe "items" or the universe "time" were treated traditionally within the concept of reliability, then the universe "situation" was so treated within the concept of validity (concurrent or predictive, depending on the case). Cone (1981b, 1987b) seems to believe that the creators of the theory of generalizability defend reliability and validity as summarizing the possibilities of generalization of a measure. Not so—in reality, the authors have tried carefully to restrict their theoretical and methodological construction in the field of reliability. But, without a doubt, the limits between reliability and validity are diminished. The problems of reliability and validity are (at least for the most part) problems of generalizability. This is already a widespread opinion among theorists (e.g., Fiske, 1978; Jackson & Paunonen, 1980; Nunnally & Durham, 1975; Wiggins, 1973) and it is also clearly seen throughout the works in behavioral assessment, including those of Cone (see also Coates & Thoresen, 1978). More precisely, between reliability and validity one can speak of a "continuum of generalizability" in which validity represents maximum generalization (Levy, 1973). This idea is explicit in the logic of Campbell and Fiske's (1959) multitrait-multimethod matrix. It is later expressed by Campbell (1960): "Reliability is agreement between measures maximally similar in method. The best examples of concurrent, predictive, and construct validity all represent agreement between highly different and independent measurement procedures" (p. 550). Fiske (1971) writes along the same line: "Reliability and validity are really on a continuum of generalizability: reliability refers to generalizing about the test as a test; validity refers to generalizing beyond the test to a concrete criterion or to a construct" (p. 172).

If classical reliability encompasses intrainstrument generalization, then validity encompasses interinstrument generalization (although not only that). But there does not seem to be any essential difference. Elsewhere, I have developed the concept of the continuum of generalizability in more detail, making reference to its possibilities and offering some necessary remarks for its adequate consideration (Silva, 1982; see also Thorndike & Hagen, 1977). Let us continue now with our line of argument.

In Raven's previously cited text, and also expressed in one form or another by several authors, there is another idea of great importance: Various indexes and facets of generalizability may be examined depending on what is to be measured. First of all, there is what one is attempting to measure and with what objective, and then there is the subordinate question of possible consistency or possible stability. This implies a consideration of consistency and stability, together with validity, within the continuum of generalizability, and **calls for the subordination of consistency and stability to validity.**[3] The issue of validity functions as the main premise: If we measure what we intend to measure and if this is considered to have a certain degree of consistency and stability, then such consistency and stability must be reproduced in the measurements. This idea is already clearly present in the work by Loevinger (1957) and has been given additional credence by other authors (e.g., Cattell, 1964, 1986; Franzen, 1989; Hattie, 1985; Haynes, 1991; Lumsden, 1976; Messick, 1989; Wiggins, 1973). "The degree of internal consistency reliability varies with the theoretical homogeneity of the construct measured by the test," writes Franzen (1989, p. 25), and the same can be said of temporal stability: "In regard to changes over time, the test-retest reliability of the scores should be commensurate with the degree of stability theoretically associated with the construct under investigation" (Messick, 1989, p. 55); "We need to substitute a concern with construct validity for our concern with even re-test reliability when we are developing assessment procedures" (Raven, 1989, p. 90). By putting traditional aspects of reliability before validity, authors bypassed the problem of consistency and stability, accepting as given what is alleged to be discovered (Silva, 1978). The subordination of consistency and stability to validity, on the other hand, puts things back into place. One of the strongest criticisms of reliability within the psychometric tradition (Lumsden, 1976) points out just this, and many authors of the behavioral movement, such as Haynes (1983) and Cone (1981b, 1987b), concur. With the theory of generalizability, and this hierarchy, we have surely taken an important step forward.

Does the Concept of Accuracy Bring Any Solution?

Some behavioral authors seem, however, to have taken a different course, turning to the concept of *accuracy.* Neither that word nor the word *precision* seems to be used by authors in a consistent way.[4] For example, Fancher (1967) uses *accuracy* to refer to the prediction of life events, distinguishing it from validity (in its theoretical sense, not its predictive one). Delclaux and Martínez Arias (n.d.) give *accuracy* a strictly psychometric sense with regard to innovative strategies for the estimation of standard measurement errors. Lord (1985), along similar lines, uses *accuracy* as a synonym of *reliability.* But Martin and Bateson (1987) take a different approach, reserving the term *precision* for the degree of random error associated with a measurement and the term *accuracy* for the degree of systematic error. The former would fall within the scope of reliability and the latter within that of validity (see also Suen & Ary, 1989). Both Nelson et al. (1977) and Weiss and Davison (1981) use the term *precision* for the comparison of a measurement with another that serves as evaluation criterion, coming closer to the meaning of *accuracy* I shall adopt here. On the other hand, it is not unusual to see the words *accuracy* and *precision* used interchangeably, as synonyms.

In his work titled "Artifact, Bias, and Complexity of Assessment: The ABCs of Reliability," Kazdin (1977a) proposes to distinguish between agreement among observers—a very old subject among applied behavior analysts—and accuracy of observation. *Accuracy* refers to the degree to which an observer's record fits a preestablished criterion about the same data. *Agreement,* on the other hand, reflects only the degree of overlap between two or more independent records; the data of one observer need not be taken as criterion. Both *accuracy* and *agreement* imply that observations are compared with some other record. The difference is in the value given to the latter as accounting target behavior. That is Kazdin's reason for a conceptual distinction. An assessor can accurately record (in relation to a preestablished criterion) and, at the same time, show limited agreement with another assessor (whose observation is inaccurate). On the contrary, he or she may record inaccurately (in relation to the criterion) and agree well with another observer (who was inaccurate in the same way).

It appears that the concept of accuracy acquired importance in behavioral science through a book by Johnston and Pennypacker (1980). According to these authors, "*Accuracy* may be defined as the extent to which obtained measures approximate values of the 'true' state of nature, perfect accuracy being obtained when equivalence is demonstrated" (p. 190). Johnston and Pennypacker begin by identifying accuracy with validity:

> The goal of any scientific measurement operation or procedure is to arrive at the best possible estimate of the true value of some dimensional quantity of a natural phenomenon. To the extent that this goal is achieved, it is said that the measurement is accurate or valid. Accuracy or validity of the results therefore becomes the yardstick for gauging the quality of any measurement procedure. (p. 190)

Nevertheless, these authors do make a distinction further on. Maintaining the traditional meaning of the term *valid,* which designates how well a measurement really reflects the object, event, or phenomenon it is supposed to measure, they state:

> In both the theory and practice of psychological measurement, distinctions are made among various kinds of validity (concurrent, construct, face, content, etc.), but all share the property of being statements about the quality of measurement that cannot be established in terms of correspondence to an independently known true value. Because such correspondence *can* be established in the case of measurement of dimensional quantities of behavior, the term *accuracy* is used instead to refer to the quality of measurement reflected by the correspondence between measured and true values. (p. 192)

Later on, the distinction is extended to reliability. *Reliability*—which had been defined as stability of measurement under constant conditions—is interpreted along the same lines as validity: It would stem from a psychometric tradition lacking accord on the very existence of the true state of things, as well as on whether or not it can be independently measured. Yet, where possible, it is accuracy that would constitute the criterion. The difference between accuracy and reliability would be conceptual, because "the means by which they are achieved and assessed at a tactical level are usually identical" (Johnston & Pennypacker, 1980, p. 195). However, it would be possible to know if the data are accurate only when the true values of the observed behavior events are known.

Johnston and Pennypacker's final reflections on the subject are disconcerting, to say the least. The entire measurement strategy and the concept of accuracy itself rest on the availability and determination of the true values. According to these authors, such values are theoretically available if the study of behavior is considered to be a natural science, as it is assumed that "all phenomena studied by the methods of the natural sciences are possessed of truly quantifiable dimensional quantities for which true values exist in each and every specific case" (p. 197). They state further that "admitting hypothetical states and processes almost ensures that measurement will be inexact, and questions of validity (not accuracy) will certainly arise" (p. 193). But, on the other hand, even if they encourage the researcher to search for accuracy, which would be generally easy and which would often yield results that are beyond all reasonable doubt, Johnston and Pennypacker also affirm that "there is always the possibility of error in any empirical measurement, and no one can ever be certain that a true value has been determined" (p. 197).

These observations seem a bit confusing. We must at least ask ourselves: If the security of working with true values will never exist and if the knowledge of them and their determination constitute the essential requisite, the *sine qua non* of the attempt to estimate the accuracy of a measurement, what is the secret path that will lead us to it?

In spite of all, the concept of accuracy has entered the field of behavior assessment with strength, particularly through the works of Cone. According to Cone, the *truth* is in fact accessible for a behavioral approach—unlike a psychometric approach that works with hypothetical constructs—insofar as the behavior is really observable. The questions that are posed in reliability and validity would be similar to those posed in behavioral assessment, with one substantial difference: "The assumption here is that the questions can be answered in a relatively absolute sense, and that measures can then be evaluated against that absolute standard or 'truth.' To the extent that they represent it faithfully they will be judged high in quality" (Cone, 1978b, p. 5). Pointing out that it is difficult to obtain this absolute standard, Cone notes that it is possible to attain it through mechanical "behavior generators" or "criterion protocols." We would thus have the criterion with which to compare our measurements and establish their accuracy.

In his 1981, 1982, and 1987 works, Cone continues to develop these ideas. He begins by defining: "The fundamental characteristic of the measurements we use to assess behavior is accuracy; that is to say, sensitivity to what is true with respect to the behavior in question" (Cone, 1987b, p. 175). *Accuracy*, which "refers to the degree to which the measurement faithfully represents the objective topographic characteristics of the behavior studied" and which implies "the agreement among data obtained with a measurement instrument and some indisputable index of the behavior in question" (Cone, 1987b, pp. 179, 182), is distinguished from *reliability*, which expresses only consistency in repeated observations. According to Cone, it is also distinguished from *validity*, which represents "the relationships between the observed behavior and some other variable or variables" (p. 180). In this way, a possible series of combinations is produced: A measurement may be reliable but not accurate, although it cannot be accurate without being reliable. A measurement can be accurate but not valid or valid but not accurate (see also Cone, 1982). Nelson (1983b) also enters this relationship game. She adopts the concept of accuracy as criterion to assess behavioral measurements in a 1983 work. Nelson shares Cone's ideas and adds a bit more: In dealing with "treatment validity" (to which we shall return in Chapter 10), she states that a measurement may be reliable, valid, and accurate without being useful. She also states the inverse: that it may be useful without being reliable, valid, or accurate! As a possible example, she cites the interview, which may prove to be useful without meeting quality standards.

When I return to the subject of utility I hope to clarify for the reader that this cannot be said rigorously, using the terms and concepts scientifically. The theory of measurement has taught us that linear relationships among reliability, validity, and utility do not exist, and yet that some degree of validity and reliability is requisite to the attainment of what has been understood as utility. To put it any other way would be to give rise to such confusion that one would be tempted to throw it all out—the baby with the bathwater, and the bathtub, if necessary.

Behavioral assessors themselves have realized the difficulties arising from the concept of accuracy as it has been defined. Hayes et al. (1986), keeping in mind Cone's (1981b, p. 57) requisite for estimating accuracy as an "incontrovertible index" against which the data are compared, note that the finding of "noncontroversial indexes" is its most serious problem. Thus "it currently has remote functional applicability to most behavioral assessment questions" (Nelson & Hayes, n.d., p. 29). Barrios (1988) makes a similar observation. Cone also recognizes that it is easy to find such indexes only for very concrete behaviors—and, I might add, perhaps not even then, where appearances tend to fool. Cone (1988) attempts to overcome the difficulty through optimism by claiming that such difficulty would, at least in part, arise from the fact that "we have not spent much time and energy on the problem" (p. 51). But can this be said?

Much effort has been made, within and outside behavioral assessment, to specify, clarify, define, and verify concrete behaviors and to place them within a rigorous process of observation and registration. Naturally, satisfactory criteria are attained often (but not absolute ones), and one immediately asks, Why not use such criteria instead of substitute measurements (Foster & Cone, 1980; Hayes et al., 1986; Nelson, 1983b), as so often occurs in prediction problems regarding the assessment of criterion variables? On the other hand, if there are many difficulties with regard to the majority of relevant, observable behaviors, then with regard to subjective behavior the issue of accuracy seems unsurmountable, as Cone (1977b) himself admits. Cone (1987b) writes that "the concepts related to accuracy of measurement are still not sufficiently developed to permit their application to private events" (p. 183).

Hayes et al. (1986) probe deeper:

> Accuracy is, in a sense, a structuralistic view of evaluating the quality of assessment. It is rare when we feel we have "incontrovertible" measures of anything, and in a philosophical sense incontrovertible standards simply do not exist. No matter how fine-grained the measurement, we always only approximate reality. (p. 496)

For these authors, the concept of accuracy is saturated not only with structuralism but also with "naive realism." Cone (1988) recognizes the possible criticism of "Platonism," but he seems to see only one epistemological alternative, an agnostic one he naturally rejects. In fact, it is true that consensus between assessors, objectivity as intersubjectivity, does not possess a simple meaning in science; this is suggested when accuracy is claimed more than consensus. Cone (1988) realizes this but does not explore the idea adequately. Surely, the concept arose (recall Kazdin, 1977a) as a protest against the somewhat frivolous and neglected practice of accepting the agreement between records, only two most of the time, accidentally collected by people without much experience or not very "independent," as an index for objectivity in observation. Of course, there are measurements that promise greater quality than others and therefore may function at a given time as criteria. No one doubts this, not even psychological assessors. But from there, to feel oneself established in the domain of truth, there is an abyss. Falling into a "physicalistic servitude," Cone proposes mechanical records as "incontrovertible" criteria. Yet, aside from the technical difficulties these may entail, and that may make them not very "accurate," Cone seems to forget that before one can use such criteria, there is a conceptual problem: defining the behavior to be measured.

This issue cannot be avoided by adducing that we are facing external, open, observable behavior. The definition of the behavior to be observed surrounds the "stream of behavior" with a conceptual halo, and this is only the beginning of many other details that go from theoretical to technical. We may believe, for example, that saying "Record the number of times that Jimmy gets up from his chair" does not result in any conceptual problem. But it does. If we analyze the movement more carefully, we realize that there are a series of possibilities and that decisions must be made. The record will be not a simple reflection of reality, but the result of decisions, agreements, or conventions having subtle aspects, such as the influence of sociocultural norms.

Remarks on accuracy move within the scope of reliability. Both Johnston and Pennypacker (1980) and Cone (1981b) recognize this. The often criticized "true value" of classic psychometrics insistently returns, but in a more naive realistic fashion. Authors go so far as to reproduce exactly as a formula for the definition of accuracy the formula for reliability: the ratio between the variance of "actual" behavior and the variance of observed scores (Cone, 1981b, 1987b). The substantialist thought that had been so criticized reappears in a supposedly new concept, only that "internal" entities are no longer referred to, but rather "external." It is now the behavior that is reified. Psychological assessment has known for some time, however, that it must work with unfinished attempts, with perspectives, with successive approaches (Cronbach, 1975), and that one cannot hope to compare measurements with absolute criteria or "truths." Rather, measurements are to be compared with other measurements; in this game there is no room for easy relativism, nor can there be absolute possession of the truth. Remarks in this vein have already been made in Peterson's (1968) book. Hogan and Nicholson (1988) also correctly point out that the so-called hard sciences face the same problem. In short, the concern for objectivity, a healthy concern that makes up the original scope of the concept of accuracy, should be viewed—like reliability—as a problem of validity (Suen, 1988; Suen & Ary, 1989; Uebersax, 1988).

Conclusion

This chapter has looked at the assumptions of consistency and stability of behavior, traditional within the psychometric standard of *reliability* and supposed by many behavioral assessors to differentiate between behavioral and psychometric approaches.

Although such assumptions did underlie theory of measurement error, recent developments in psychometrics view reliability as belonging to measurement and consistency and stability as attributes of behavior, present in a greater or lesser degree. It follows that validity has priority: The most reliable score will not be the most consistent and stable, but rather the one that best reflects the attributes of what ought to be measured.

The concept of *accuracy,* introduced in an attempt to overcome supposed problems with reliability and validity, deserves severe criticism. It led Johnston and Pennypacker (1980) to a dead end and reintroduced a naive realistic epistemology, leading toward dogmatism. Problems of accuracy may be better understood within the concepts of reliability and validity, which constitute its original framework. The theory of generalizability helps us to take a definitive step toward unifying reliability and validity, freeing the concept of reliability from any substantialist temptation. The theoretical contributions of this approach deserve the attention of all behavioral assessors.

Notes

1. Kendall (1985) speaks similarly of temporal stability. He criticizes Nelson's (1983a) simple rejection of stability, a rejection that has little to do with empirical evidence (e.g., Mischel, 1983, 1984a).

2. In Cattell's ideas on reliability we also find a strong rejection of the traditional notion of internal consistency—condemned as an "itemetric" approach—as well as of the traditional valuation of temporal stability (see, for instance, Cattell, 1964, 1970, 1986; Cattell & Tsujioka, 1964; Hattie, 1985; Morales, 1988).

3. Cronbach et al. (1972) point this out: "Because a study of consistency among samples of behavior challenges or confirms the investigator's working concept of the variable, it is a part of instrument validation as well as a study of instrument precision" (p. 6).

4. This lack of accord can be seen in an interesting and recent reexamination of the concept of accuracy by Suen (1988).

6

THE CONCEPT OF VALIDITY

Validity has had growing importance in psychometrics, and has become the central concept of standards of quality (Cronbach, 1984a). One early text that mentioned this is worth looking at. In 1937, Monroe observed that there was

> 1. a growing emphasis upon validity and a consequent decreasing emphasis upon reliability as the criterion for evaluating measuring instruments;
> 2. a decline of the faith in indirect measurement and an increasing emphasis upon direct measurement as a means of attaining satisfactory validity. (quoted in Haney, 1981, p. 1023)

Much the same thought was expressed a decade later by the authors of the famous report of the Office of Strategic Services (1948): "In retrospect it seems a little peculiar that for thirty years we psychologists should have devoted so much time to improving the reliability of our tests and so little time to improving their validity" (pp. 142-143). Now, some decades later, Schoenfeldt (1984) has written: "The future of validation research is promising. There has been more progress in the last decade than in the previous quarter century. Extending this trajectory will undoubtedly lead to new learning about the inferential value of tests in predicting and understanding behavior" (pp. 81-82; see also Angoff, 1988, for a review of the evolution of the concept that gathers many aspects to be discussed below).

As validity is one of the slipperiest and most multifaceted concepts in social science methodology (Matesanz, 1975), we must attempt to pinpoint it, adhering to the strictest possible psychometric perspective. Vernon (1964/1966) summarizes the tradition. Several definitions, he says, indicate that a test is essentially valid as long as it detects and measures what it alleges to measure and not something else (e.g., Angoff, 1988; Carmines & Zeller, 1979; Thorndike & Hagen, 1977). This definitional line is maintained today (e.g., Martin & Bateson, 1987). True though this statement is, this chapter must also recognize briefly an important evolution within the concept of validity.

Vernon (1964/1966) himself made a significant advance:

> We intend to argue a somewhat more unorthodox view—that a test measures only itself, but that it is valid in so far as it can be shown to correlate with other observable behaviour. That is, its validity lies in the *inferences* we are entitled to make from it. (p. 407; emphasis added)

He further stated:

> Fundamentally . . . a test measures itself, and its further validity rests entirely on its established relations to other behaviours. It is the network of its relations to other variables and . . . life situations that gives its meaning. (p. 412)

This interpretive line, though it seemed somewhat heterodox to Vernon, is in close accord with the idea of construct validation (see Chapter 9) and of the first *Standards* (APA, 1954, Norm C2). *Validation* refers to the determination of appropriateness for all the interpretations made of a test score: descriptive, explicative, and predictive. Cronbach (1971) suggests that "to study the validity of a test interpretation is to study how behavior in one situation is related to behavior in another" (p. 448). These observations (also made by other authors, e.g., Anastasi, 1986; Guion, 1974; Schoenfeldt, 1984) are recognized in the 1974 *Standards,* which in that sense surpass those of 1966. The definition is clear and succinct: "Validity refers to the appropriateness of inferences from test scores or other forms of assessment" (APA, AERA, & NCME, 1974, p. 25). The 1985 *Standards* follow the same direction in this respect. *Validity* is defined as "the degree to which a certain inference from a test is appropriate or meaningful," and *validation* as "the process of investigation by which the degree of validity of a proposed test interpretation can be evaluated" (AERA, APA, & NCME, 1985, p. 94). Campbell (1960) was right, in a comment on the first *Standards,* that in the absence of an interpretive intention the question of validity does not arise and requirements for it cannot be stated.

If validity is attached to interpretations, then it is not the instrument that is validated: "The phrase *validation of a test* is a source of much misunderstanding. One validates, not a test, but an *interpretation of data arising from a specified procedure*" (Cronbach, 1971, p. 447; see also Binning & Barrett, 1989; Franzen, 1989; García Ramos, 1986; Messick, 1989; Morales, 1988; Nunnally, 1978; Rubin, 1988). Cronbach and Quirk (1976) write further: "There is no such thing as 'the' validity of a test. No test is valid for all purposes, in all situations, and for all groups" (p. 165). The degree of validity always depends on the particular use, hence one must always ask, Validity for what? (Garcia Ramos, 1986; Haynes, 1991; Novick, 1984). Moreover, validity is something alive, something that cannot be locked into given data by the instrument manual. Validity is not a question of all or nothing. The question is reopened with each new use of an instrument and so has no end (Anastasi, 1986; Brinberg & McGrath, 1985; Cronbach, 1989; García Ramos, 1986; Messick, 1989; Morales, 1988; Nunnally, 1978; Nunnally & Durham, 1975; Suen & Ary, 1989). Regarding this, the *Standards* speak with almost provocative clarity:

> It is important to note that validity is itself inferred, not measured. Validity coefficients may be presented in a manual, but validity for a particular aspect of test use is inferred from this collection of coefficients. It is, therefore, something that is judged as adequate, or marginal, or unsatisfactory. (APA, AERA, & NCME, 1974, p. 25)

In reality, it is the use that makes a test more or less valid, within a complex process of assessment that includes more than just the "naked instrument": "The instrument . . . is only one element in a procedure, and a validation study examines the procedure as a whole. Every aspect of the setting in which the test is given and every detail of the procedure may have an influence on performance and hence on what is measured" (Cronbach, 1971, p. 449; see also Anastasi et al., 1984). In short, the person responsible for valid use of an instrument is the person who interprets and uses it—a remark already present in the first edition of the *Standards* (APA, 1954). The interpretation must consider the published data and also the concrete situation of the measurement, including aspects ranging from the physical to the cultural and evaluative.

This more realistic and concrete interpretation of what is meant by validity and validation could be thought to reinforce the distinction between "types" of validity. Just the opposite has happened (Cronbach, 1980). Because the use and interpretation of instruments can serve varied goals, there can be very diverse validation strategies. Still, the concept of validity is essentially **unitary**. In his 1980 work, Messick vigorously defends this idea: "Different kinds of inferences from test scores require different kinds of evidence, not different kinds of validity. . . . Although it may prove helpful conceptually to discuss the interdependent features of the generic concept in terms of different aspects or facets, it is simplistic to think of different types or kinds of validity" (p. 1014; see also Messick, 1989). For Messick and for others, the innumerable "validities" that have appeared over the years misdirect thought. The strategy should be described, not labeled (e.g., content relevance or content representativeness instead of content validity). The *Standards,* which began by pointing out the triad of validities labeled "criterion-oriented validity"/"content validity"/"construct validity" (which Guion, 1980, has called the "holy trinity of validity"), have been sensitive to the evolution toward unity, especially in the latest edition: "Although evidence may be accumulated in many ways, validity always refers to the degree to which that evidence supports the inferences that are made from the scores" (AERA, APA, & NCME, 1985, p. 9). The categories "criterion," "content," and "construct" may be convenient, but they do not imply sharp distinctions. They are not "types of validity," nor do they correspond precisely to separate types of inference or use of instruments (see also Binning & Barrett, 1989; Tenopyr & Oeltjen, 1982).

Authors such as Anastasi et al. (1984) were pleased with the unitary and flexible focus in the new 1985 *Standards* that, putting such categories in their right places, avoided much confusion and misunderstanding. For other authors, such as Landy (1986), the emendation that appears in the 1985 *Standards* is still insufficient. He would emphasize even more the unitary nature of validity. There should be no limit on concrete validation procedures, but beyond this variety the process of validation is always the same, identified with the scientific process of hypothesis testing. This central observation inspired Cronbach's ideas on validity (e.g., Cronbach, 1971) as well as those of Messick (1989): "Inferences are hypotheses, and the validation of inferences is hypotheses testing" (pp. 13-14). "Remember, test validation is in essence hypothesis testing" (p. 41). And Guion (1976) states more radically: "The problem is not one of evaluating tests, it is one of developing and validating hypotheses" (quoted in Messick, 1989, p. 64; see also Landy, 1986). We shall come back to this point.

A final issue follows: On the one hand, to validate means to check the appropriateness of an inference, and there are no watertight divisions inside validation; on the other hand, any type of data may be useful.

Anything, from the behavior of the items of instruments or assessment strategies to reliability data or to correlations with criteria, may be used. Anastasi (1986) summarizes this widely expressed idea:

> Almost any information gathered in the process of developing or using a test is relevant to its validity. It is relevant in the sense that it contributes to our understanding of what the test measures. . . . If we think of test validity in terms of understanding what a particular test measures, it should be apparent that virtually any empirical data obtained with the test represent a potential source of validity information. (p. 3; see also Anastasi, 1988; Suen & Ary, 1989; further, see Haynes, 1978, in the framework of behavioral assessment)

This remark does slip into the incorrect expression "test validity," although Anastasi herself has disavowed it elsewhere. Conscious though I am of the essentially unitary character of validity, the next chapters do take up criterion-related, content, and construct validity seriation, with the aim of ordering the debate and better analyzing what has been said with regard to validity in behavioral assessment.

Conclusion

The current psychometric concept continues faithful to the tradition: Validity expresses the degree to which an instrument measures what it alleges to measure and not something else. This thought has been amplified in this chapter in important respects:

1. Validity is associated with the *inferences* that are made after obtaining scores with an instrument in particular circumstances.
2. It is not the instrument that is validated but rather the interpretations made after scoring.
3. Validity itself is a judgment, reached after compiling all information, and not reducible to a coefficient or coefficients.
4. "Types" and "classes" of validity are misnomers for types and classes of argument. The concept of validity is essentially *unitary*.
5. There is no limit to the range of data used to estimate validity. Any information may be relevant in a validation process, which is the scientific process of hypothesis construction and testing.

We can accept, as a more recent and integrative definition than those traditionally quoted, the one Messick (1989) puts forward: "Validity is an integrated evaluative judgement of the degree to which empirical evidence and theoretical rationales support the *adequacy* and *appropriateness* of *inferences* and *actions* based on test scores or other modes of assessment" (p. 13).

CHAPTER

7

CRITERION-RELATED
VALIDITY

T his chapter's focus is criterion-oriented validity in behavioral assessment. This psychometric concept has been defined as follows:

> Criterion-related validity is the extent to which scores on one variable, usually a predictor, may be used to infer performance on a different and operationally independent variable called a criterion. (Guion, 1974, p. 288)

A criterion is no more than a variable that one hopes to predict. A variable may take the role of predictor in one case (e.g., academic performance as predictor of professional performance) and the role of a criterion in another (e.g., the same academic performance predicted by an intelligence test). Criterion-related validation examines straightforward "convergence of indicators" (Cronbach, 1971; see also Haynes, 1983). Understood in its methodological sense as covariation, prediction can be *pre*dictive, *para*dictive, or *post*dictive (e.g., Cattell, 1986; Nunnally, 1978; Nunnally

& Durham, 1975). Its etymological sense limits the term to *prediction*, in relation to the future. In order to avoid this double meaning of the term *prediction*, the APA, in the 1966 *Standards*, replaced the original expression "predictive validity" with "criterion-related validity." This does not deny the practical importance of distinguishing between *concurrent* (paradictive) and *predictive* (forward-looking) validity.

Criterion-oriented validity, identified with the traditional diagnostic approach, is rejected by many behavioral assessors. The reason is simple: Behavioral assessment directly evaluates criterion variables. Two fundamental works in this discipline by Mischel (1968) and Goldfried and Kent (1972) show how prediction is impoverished as predictive variables move away from the criteria. The opposite path must be taken. The variables assessed should be those that will be included in the intervention program (Hersen, 1976). The conclusion is clear: "To the extent that the criterion situation and the test situation are one and the same, generalizability is not an issue, and questions of [criterion-related] validity are thus by definition meaningless" (Goldfried & Linehan, 1977, p. 21). Such thinking minimizes the usefulness of the predictor/criterion distinction in behavioral assessment (Cone, 1988; Hayes et al., 1986).

"Other authors do not agree with this infraevaluation of the role of this type of validity" (Martínez Arias, 1981, p. 181). For example, Goldfried and Linehan (1977) add that criterion-related validity can be a concern when indirect measurements and experimental analogues are used. They complain that "surprisingly little research has been done on the criterion-related validity of these procedures" (p. 22). Along this same line, in reviewing the results of such a typical behavioral assessment technique as role play, Kendall (1984, 1985) points out that much could be learned if we were to look closely at what our psychological colleagues in charge of personnel selection have done. It is frankly utopian to think that direct observation and recording are always possible in the natural environment. This approach to data is also expensive and subject to bias and distortion. The use of self-monitoring as complementary to direct observation in natural environments does not solve the problem (aside from creating other problems related to the quality of the assessment). A major reason for the frequent use of indirect measurements and analogues, common in professional praxis and in behavioral assessment research (e.g., Staats & Fernández-Ballesteros, 1988), stems from those difficulties.

Given that practical necessity of indirect assessment is justified on practical grounds, then it requires empirical and theoretical support. Within the limits of radical or operant behaviorism, there would be no possible justification (Burns, 1980; Staats, 1975, 1986). This handicap originally extended into behavioral assessment:

One of the basic assumptions underlying behavioral assessment *is that the behavioral sample measures nothing beyond itself* (Goldfried & Sprafkin, 1974; Mischel, 1968, 1972).[1] . . . The logical outcome of this assumption is that there is no theoretical rationale for the employment of an indirect sample of behavior (interviews, self-report inventories, standardized tests, etc.) to make decisions about another non-sampled population of behaviors. (Burns, 1980, p. 197)

Given that indirect assessment is carried on and has many times been effective, it is logical to seek a theoretical base. Staats and Burns propose such a base by opening up the theory of behavior to personality, which is simultaneously conceptualized as "basic behavioral repertoires" that would codetermine actual behavior. In that sense, Staats and others see paradigmatic behaviorism as especially suitable for behavioral assessment.

If one's *units of analysis* are broader than those in the molecular focus of radical behaviorism, criterion-oriented validity becomes relevant too. As noted in Chapter 1, the units of analysis, objects of both study and treatment, have recently been considered in a more molar way. We are already far from regarding molecular and isolated behavior as the objective of assessment and therapy. We should deal with groups of responses, related and organized among themselves. This is another of the aspects that paradigmatic behaviorism and its concept of "basic behavioral repertoire" explicitly want to attain and is also the principal reason behavioral assessment has decidedly approached the descriptive-syndromatic focus present in the latest psychopathological classifications, especially in the DSM-III and DSM-III-R (American Psychiatric Association, 1987). As Nelson (1987) acknowledges, "The single strongest factor in the increasing acceptance by behavioral assessors of diagnostic classification in general, and of DSM-III in particular, is the recognition of response covariation within the behavioral repertoires of individuals" (p. 316; see also Haynes & O'Brien, 1988; Hersen, 1988; Hersen & Bellack, 1988b; Nelso & Maser, 1988).

Kazdin (1985) suggests that questions about concurrent and predictive validity are the most important questions of validity to be confronted by the behavioral assessor. His suggestion deals with another aspect of criterion-oriented validity that a behavioral approach must take into account: prediction of future behavior, where the *prediction of the results of the intervention* has a preeminent status. Turkat (1982) states it clearly: "In preintervention assessment, our goal is to develop a formulation that utilizes the client's history and current problem dimensions to predict future behavior" (p. 252), and Kendall (1984) says that studies of criterion-oriented validity should be concerned with predicting the degree of success expected from the planned intervention. Upon careful observation, this is not a departure from the psychometric idea of criterion-oriented validity. When we deal with the prediction of a person's performance in a concrete workplace, or when we deal with the prediction of the success that a specific therapy will have with a client, we have exactly the same problem. In both cases, we must find the optimum Aptitude × Treatment interaction, which Cronbach (1957) outlined as the central task of psychological testing (e.g., Silva, 1980).

Psychometric and behavioral assessment follow the same path when they seek to predict criterion behaviors. At the beginning of this chapter we saw that behavioral assessment is concerned with assessing criterion variables themselves, prior to planning intervention. It is assumed that this immediately works toward an improvement of prediction. With respect to this point, Mischel (1972, p. 323) states that predictive validity decreases when predictive behavior and criterion behavior become less similar. Therefore, the behavior used to predict should be as similar as possible to the criterion behavior.

Is this issue alien to the psychometric approach? By no means. Recall Monroe's remark of 1937 quoted in Chapter 6. The following lines are from Cronbach and Gleser's classic book, originally published in 1957:

> High validity coefficients have most often been attained for tests which are essentially work samples of their criteria. A typing test given an applicant, a test of mathematical ability given a prospective engineering student—these tests offer good validity because they reproduce the criterion situation in miniature. . . . *Per contra,* tests having rather low zero-order validities often deal with attributes that are hard to test, and also hard to assess from any non-test data. Tests of leadership, social and emotional adjustment, or creativeness rarely boast validity coefficients beyond .30. (Cronbach & Gleser, 1965, pp. 35-36)

"To the criteria themselves"—paraphrasing the Husserlian "to the things themselves"—is then (of course, to the extent that it is possible) a common expression in psychometric as well as behavioral assessment. However, the former also brings up a problem connected with prediction, which we will consider now.

The problem deals with the tendency to approach prediction with blind empiricism or positivism, so to speak. As a matter of fact, studies of criterion-related validity tended during several decades to rely on a weak, even practically nonexistent, theoretical base for both predictive and criterion variables. This fact was responsible for the failures in prediction, and has been insistently denounced (see, e.g., Ghiselli, 1955, 1966; Silva, 1982). It is a basis of Cronbach and Meehl's 1955 article and, likewise, of the following APA *Standards* (Landy, 1986). Kelly (1955) was one of the first to protest against "mere prediction" that does not show an understanding of behavior (e.g., Hogan & Nicholson, 1988; Lamiell, Trierweiler, & Foss, 1983). In his review of assessment theory and techniques, Wittenborn (1957) spoke of a "refreshing tendency" to flee from the exclusively empirical (predictive) validations, together with a greater concern for the conceptual validity of procedures. Loevinger (1957) strongly criticized criterion-oriented validation, calling it a strictly ad hoc and "administrative" approach that lacks a scientific base; it ought not be called validation at all (see also Schoenfeldt, 1984). Anastasi, who also reacted strongly against the atheoreticism that has been dominant in psychological assessment (see Anastasi, 1967), reminds us, in a recent work, that excessive empiricism hampers practice:

> Under conditions of blind empiricism, test validity may drop to virtually zero in cross-validation—there are some dramatic demonstrations of this fact in the literature (Kurz, 1948; Cureton, 1950). Shrinkage can be drastically reduced, however, when items are prepared to fit clearly formulated hypotheses derived from psychological theory or from previous investigations of criterion requirements (Primoff, 1952). It is apparent that clear construct definition as a guide to item writing is not only logically defensible but also efficient. (Anastasi, 1986, p. 6)

Attempting to understand prediction allows us to see criterion validity through the eyes of construct validity. This is precisely what Loevinger (1957) claims as a way of recovering its scientific status, and is also stated by Cronbach (1971):

> The evidence from a single criterion-oriented validation pins down a fact about a particular local situation. That study, like every other study involving the test, helps to amplify the picture of what the test means and how it relates to the demands of nontest situations. . . . As they accumulate, therefore, criterion-oriented studies play the same role as do other studies pertinent to construct validation. (p. 503)

In short, as Messick (1981b) puts it, constructs are the bridges joining predictors and criteria: "Neither the criterion nor the predictor can be taken for granted; both should be analyzed in construct terms and preferably conjointly. Thus, the analysis of predictor measures within the framework of the criterion's construct network, and vice versa, provides a powerful, rational basis for criterion prediction" (pp. 11-12; see also Binning & Barrett, 1989; Messick, 1989). It is then clear that construct validity provides the "rational foundation for predictive validity" (Guion, 1976; quoted in Messick, 1980, p. 1013), and that criterion-oriented validity and construct validity have a part-whole relationship (Morales, 1988). In the context of criterion-referenced testing, Haertel (1985) arrives at the same conclusion: "The necessity of making inferences to a broader domain than the test directly samples brings a need for some deeper theoretical basis for linking test and criterion. This is a need for construct validation" (p. 25). A scientific prediction requires an explanation, and this explanation—by being a maximum force of prediction—empowers the prediction itself. The maxim "There is nothing more useful than a good theory" is pertinent.

Prediction through constructs—taken by Taft (1959/1971) as an "analytical model" of prediction, different from a "naive empirical" and a "global" or intuitive one—has been a controversial subject. Meehl (1959/1973a, 1979) has pointed out that mature scientific conditions have not being achieved in clinical psychology, and hence construct-mediated predictions cannot be really efficient. In the first stages of behavioral assessment, construct-mediated prediction was also rejected, as in a book by Mischel (1968) and an article by Goldfried and Kent (1972). Recent attitudes are not so extreme, however. Thus, for example, Haynes (1983) defines criterion-referenced validity as "the degree to which data from an assessment instrument correlate with data from another assessment instrument *presumed to measure the same or a similar construct*" (p. 405; emphasis added).

We saw at the beginning of this chapter that a common desire of behavioral and psychometric assessment is to come as close as possible to the criteria themselves—to attain, within the realm of the possible, predictors that are more than "miniatures," samples of criterion behaviors. This has led many behavioral assessors to establish *content* validity as one of the most important concerns with regard to validity, to the detriment of criterion-oriented validity and of construct validity. They insist on contrasting a "sample approach" and a "sign approach." All this obliges us to turn on content validity, attempting to unravel its methodological status and its place within a unitary conception of validity. It is possible that content validation and construct validation are not as distant as some think.

Conclusions

The issue of criterion-oriented validity—which might have been overcome in behavioral assessment by identifying predictors with criteria—remains. The predictor-criterion approach is not an exclusive characteristic of behavioral assessment; rather, it is present in both the origins and most recent evolutions of psychometric assessment.

The questions regarding criterion-oriented validity are established in behavioral assessment by different motives and in different aspects. Primarily, they are established to the extent that the identification of predictor with criterion is more *desideratum* than reality. In behavioral assessment, there is much room for so-called indirect methods. However, the most important route continues to be identical to that established in psychometric assess ent: that of *the prediction of treatment results.*

As a matter of fact, by understanding treatment in its broadest sense, psychological assessment has as its target what Cronbach stated in his 1957 article: to find the optimum Aptitude × Treatment interaction for each case.

An evolution in the consideration of criterion-oriented validity seems to be common in psychometric and behavioral approaches to assessment. We now see attempts to interpret predictions in relation to psychological processes. This conception means the inclusion of evidence on predictors and criteria within the hierarchically superior concept of construct validity.

Note

1. To state this another way: Only an evaluative focus that refers to samples is accepted. This will be addressed in the next chapter.

8

CONTENT VALIDITY

Behavioral assessors agree on the need for and importance of content validity. If there has been more or less controversy with regard to other standards, concern for ensuring the content validity of instruments has been universal.

M. R. Goldfried (1981) and M. M. Linehan (1980) have been those most concerned with this topic. Goldfried quotes the *Standards* of APA, AERA, and NCME (1974): "Evidence of content validity is required when the test user wishes to estimate how an individual performs in the universe of situations the test is intended to represent" (p. 28). Linehan quotes Anastasi (1976), for whom content validity "involves essentially the systematic examination of the test content to determine whether it covers a representative sample of the behavior domain to be measured" (pp. 134-135).

The concern for content validity is closely related to the "criterion-reference" focus characteristic of behavioral assessment, discussed in Chapter 4 (see Linehan, 1980; Martínez Arias, 1981). Considering the test as a sample of a defined set of behaviors, content validation essentially deals with sample population representativeness. We must recognize, however, that representativeness has been treated in more than one way. Anastasi's definition, which guides Linehan (1980), speaks of a "behavior domain" in tune with the original approach of criterion-referenced tests. Other authors speak, along this same line, of "tasks" or "performances" (e.g., Guion, 1974; Schoenfeldt, 1984). However, Linehan (1980) himself, commenting on Livingston (1977), says later that content validity deals with the determination of "how well the conditions under which the person's behavior is actually observed represent all those sets of conditions to which one is interested in generalizing" (p. 149). This is along the same line as the definition in the *Standards,* cited by Goldfried, which mentions the representativeness of a "universe of situations" (although the same *Standards* also speak of "behaviors"). Goldfried and Linehan (1977) speak of a situational representativeness and also of a temporal stability. Surely, stability should remain within the concept of reliability so as not to mix things excessively. The other aforementioned aspects have been repeatedly pointed out in references to content validity (Cronbach, 1984a; Fitzpatrick, 1983): the items or elements of which an instrument is made (including instructions and other determinants) as representative of a universe of stimuli or of a situational universe, and the responses that the instrument elicits as representative of a behavioral universe. A good sign of this double concern in the area of content validity within behavioral assessment is that the procedure cited as paradigmatic to its determination, proposed by Goldfried and D'Zurilla (1969), includes a "*situational* analysis" and a "*response* enumeration" and "evaluation" (see Goldfried, 1977, 1981; Martínez Arias, 1981). It is precisely because of this double aspect of content validity (Goldfried & Davison, 1976) that Strosahl and Linehan (1986) view it as especially important in an approach such as the behavioral one, which emphasizes the functional relationship between stimulus and response.

Not without reason, content validity has been seriously questioned in some developments of the psychometric approach (Morales, 1988). For Thorndike (1966), to speak of "content sampling" is strange to say the least, and leads to confusion. For Loevinger (1957, 1965), to speak of a sampling from a population of contents is an abusive extension of the concept of sampling. Other authors, including Guion (1977), Tenopyr (1977), Fitzpatrick (1983), and Klauer (1984), have published monographs on the subject or have dedicated important sections to it (e.g., Messick, 1975, 1989; Morales, 1988). The widespread conclusion is that applying the word *validity* to a sampling of test contents, that is, of stimuli, is incorrect, as it provides no evidence on the interpretation of scores or responses. This idea was, to a certain extent, already present in the first *Standards*: "The user cannot judge, from [content] alone, how well the test permits drawing conclusions about any form of behavior other than the test behavior" (APA, 1954, p. 20). It would be better, it is said, to speak of representativeness, relevance, or clarity of content.[1]

If "content validity" deals with representativeness and relevance of responses in test scores, we are, without a doubt, in the realm of validity. Messick (1975) quotes an old text by Lennon (1956), who proposed a definition of content validity: "The extent to which a subject's responses to the items of a test may be considered to be a representative sample of his responses to a real or hypothetical universe of situations which together constitute the area of concern to the person interpreting the test" (p. 295). But, if this is so—and it would extend to samplings of content (items) or situations—content validity falls within construct validity and is to be seen in that perspective (Anastasi, 1986; Drenth, 1969; Fitzpatrick, 1983; Guion, 1974; Messick, 1975, 1980, 1988, 1989). For Tenopyr (1977), "At the minimum, content validity may be considered propaedeutic to construct validation. At the maximum, content validity may be assumed to be one type of evidence to construct validity" (p. 51; see Cronbach, 1971; Fiske, 1971). For Guion (1977, p. 4) a sampling of behaviors within a defined domain of contents, with its specific set of operations, could constitute the operative definition of a construct (see also Kerlinger, 1973).[2]

Loevinger (1957) referred to this point when she proposed to place content validity within that part of construct validity that she called "substantive validity." A simple question will clarify: What can limit the universe of contents and determine the importance of each subarea, except the scientific concept that serves as a base? (See Drenth, 1969; Gómez Benito, 1986; Messick, 1989; Silva, 1982.) Note that Cronbach (1971) insistently protests the use of correlational consistency or homogeneity in the context of content validity: If the defined universe of contents is heterogeneous, a low degree of homogeneity is consistent with validity (see also Wiggins, 1973). To represent a construct is to share its characteristics, among which there may be a specified homogeneity. How can these remarks not remind us of remarks made by Raven (1966) and other authors on internal consistency and temporal stability? It seems that in order to evaluate metric quality it is necessary to examine the scientific concepts in play, implying a close link to construct validity.

There is a second reason for linking content validity to construct validity, which also serves to lead us away from a static view of the latter. Lennon (1956) attempts to get to the heart of the concept:

> Content validity is ascribed to the subject's responses rather than to the test questions themselves . . . to underscore the point that appraisal of content validity must take into account not only the *content* of the questions but also

the *process* presumably employed by the subject in arriving at his response. (p. 296)

As a matter of fact, if the attempt to explain the responses—the behavioral performance, in its broadest sense—carries us beyond a strictly stimulus-response consideration to the postulation of some type of psychological process, the argument illustrates what was once known as "the validation of working hypotheses" (Cronbach, 1972). In the words of Messick (1980), "The important sampling consideration in test construction is not representative-ness of the surface content of tasks but representativeness of the processes employed by subjects in arriving at a response" (p. 1018). Messick (1975) also notes, "This concern with the processes underlying test responses places this approach to content validity squarely in the realm of construct validity" (p. 961).

Finally, there is a third reason for linking content validity to construct validity. In content validation, it is agreed that sampling from a domain or universe is almost always nonrandom or "systematic" (e.g., Cronbach, 1971; Rubin, 1988). If this means differential weighting, a hierarchical estimate of the areas within the set of possible contents with the intent of representing them in the instrument in proper proportion, we have neces-sarily entered the evaluative level. Nunnally and Durham, among others, convincingly develop this observation: "Values determine the relative stress on different types of content" (Nunnally & Durham, 1975, p. 295; see also Messick, 1989; Nunnally 1978). Values pervade the concept of validity and all attempts at validation.

The development of psychometric thought is made clear if we consider, on the one hand, that certain constructions called content validation do not answer a question of validity truly or totally and, on the other hand, that those constructions that do answer a question of validity fit better within the framework of construct validity. When behavioral assessors look at the relation between the two aspects of validity, they move away from the slogans that seem to oppose these two aspects and decidedly move toward the view current in psychometrics. Thus Linehan (1980), in the only monograph I know of in behavioral assessment to be dedicated to content validation, reminds us that one of the reasons for emphasizing its necessity is the attempt to measure behavioral constructs. Concretely, Linehan sees the process of validation as follows:

> Once the conceptual definition for a construct has been determined, an important validity question is whether the sample of both stimuli and re-sponses observed and recorded during the measurement procedure is a representative sample of the behavior universe which conceptually defines

the construct in question. (p. 151; see also Cone, 1982; Haynes, 1991; Suen & Ary, 1989)

Perhaps if the words "conceptual" and "conceptually" were replaced with *operational* and *operationally*—which seem more fitting—this statement could have been written by any of the psychometrically oriented authors cited above. If behavioral assessment emphasizes content validation and the traditional approach emphasizes construct validation, that happens, Linehan says, because the former works with less abstract constructs and gives them no explanatory-causal function. For Linehan, behavioral constructs come closer to what are called "intervening variables" (see also Goldfried, 1977; Goldfried & Linehan, 1977). In the following chapter I shall return to these remarks, with which I do not completely agree. I do agree with Linehan that the two types of validation face the same problems. Thus, for example, it has been also clear for some time in behavioral assessment that in content validation, we necessarily evaluate: The third stage of the schema proposed by Goldfried and D'Zurilla (1969) refers precisely to this.

Sample and Signs

Before ending this chapter, it seems appropriate to touch upon a topic discussed in behavioral assessment: *sample-oriented* and *sign-oriented* approaches. Goldfried and Kent (1972) recall the distinction made by Goodenough (1949) between *sample* and *sign*. Behavior is considered to be a sign when it is understood as an indirect manifestation of underlying personality characteristics. Behavior is considered to be a sample when what is observed is a subgroup or sample of the behaviors of interest. Therefore, content validation—that is, the attainment of representative behavior samples—moves to a superior position within behavioral assessment.

The sign/sample distinction has been broadly accepted. Almost no comparison of behavioral with traditional assessment fails to ascribe a sample orientation to the former and a sign orientation to the latter. Moreover, this polarity seems to be gaining greater importance (e.g., Barrios, 1988).

Sundberg, Tyler, and Taplin (1973; see also Sundberg, 1977) complicate matters by adding an orientation toward "correlates" to the two previously mentioned. They refer to functioning at a middle level of inference between the low level of samples and the high level of signs: The inference "rests on the assumption of *relationship*, thus associating that being assessed with 'something' different. Therefore, if a subject with psycho-motor slowness claims to be sad and eat little, the psychologist infers that he is depressed; the term depression is used as a *descriptive generalization* and no more" (Fernández-Ballesteros, 1983b, p. 56; see also Bernstein & Nietzel, 1982).

The sign orientation is more ambitious:

> When used as a sign, an observation is seen as something more than a correlate. It is fundamentally related to a person's nature, it is a pointer to an inner condition, symbolic of a larger personal process. The assessing person is using a "hypothetical construct" about the personality in guessing that the glum silence is a sign of a personality condition such as fear of sex. (Sundberg, 1977, pp. 23-24)

The sign approach thus refers to personality structures (Messick, 1981a) and not to response classes (as the sample approach does); it refers to underlying traits (Martínez Arias, 1981), to a *"hypothetical construct* or internal state which implies an etiology or causal condition with an intrapsychic base" (Fernández-Ballesteros, 1983b, p. 56).[3]

Therefore, it really stands out that an author such as Cronbach, inspired also by Goodenough, sees things in a different way. First, he does not consider the "correlate" level for the simple reason that the correlate would characterize the sign approach:

> The sign approach treats a test response as behavior for which interesting correlates have been identified. The correlations are established empirically (that is, "from experience"). . . . Any description that does not stick close to the kind of behavior observed is a "sign" interpretation. (Cronbach, 1984a, pp. 465-466)

He therefore associates criterion-referenced validity with the sign approach, a sign being no more than an "indicator" of *behaviors different* from those of the test (see Cronbach, 1984a, p. 88). Wiggins (1973) expresses the same idea, citing Goodenough (1949) and Loevinger (1957): "In viewing an observed behavior as a sign . . . one assumes that it is an 'indicant' of criterion behaviors which may be topographically quite dissimilar" (p. 307). The sign may refer to "internal states" but also to "other behaviors" (Cronbach, 1984a, p. 45; see also Wiggins, 1973). Whereas the sign approach is identified with the actuarial approach, it can be said that the trait perspective is closer to samples than to signs (see Cronbach, 1984a, pp. 455, 465).

We can best return to the instigator and creator of this distinction: Goodenough (1949). While speaking about projective techniques, she says that we must shift the focus from that her book had applied to other techniques, such as psychometric instruments of intelligence. In those tests and in self-reports, Goodenough says, behavior samples are gathered that "are assumed to be representative of the larger areas of similar abilities, behaviors, and claims from which the samples have presumably been drawn" (p. 83). In projective techniques the behavior is seen as a sign, since "it is of the very nature of a sign that its overt character does not necessarily resemble the thing signified" (p. 83).

The above leads Goodenough to conclude that traits are probably closer to a sample approach and that the sign approach is tied to problems of *prediction* (see Goodenough, 1989, p. 100). Only through these remarks are we able to understand Goodenough's table comparing the "method of samples" with the "method of signs." Had it not been written by her, many people would have thought that the headings had been reversed (see Table 8.1).

How could one better characterize a trait focus than to say that the universe is predefined, has arbitrary limits, and usually works with abstract nouns, and that interpretations of terminology vary with different workers? Here, these phrases are attached to the method of samples. On the other hand, the method of signs is empirical, objective, and tied to behavior. Thus when Goodenough places the projective techniques within the sign approach it is **not** because of their frequent reference to intrapsychic entities, as one might think, but rather because of the *topographical* contrast between behavior during a test and the behaviors the test claims to predict. In reality, Goodenough makes no reference to hypothetical constructs, intrapsychic states, underlying traits that cause or explain behavior, or anything of this sort. The method of signs falls into the field of what later came to be called criterion-related validity, emphasizing its required empirical character. It is from there that the correlates may be envisioned within a sign approach (Goodenough, 1949, p. 102).

I am therefore obliged to agree with Wiggins and Cronbach, not with Goldfried and Kent and many others, in the interpretation they make of Goodenough's sign/sample distinction. Goldfried and Kent cite Goodenough but seem not to follow her; their inspiration comes probably from Mischel (1968; see also Messick, 1989; Wernimont & Campbell, 1968), who, at several places in his book, makes the distinction in terms inconsistent with Goodenough. In reality, the only part of Goodenough's original distinction that is retained is that the sample orientation sticks as closely as possible to a determined type of behavior—nothing more.

At this point it is relevant to take a look once again at the relation between content and construct validity. Goodenough clearly realizes that a "method of samples" cannot function without conceptual support, without a scientific construction that marks the boundaries and gives it meaning. That is why the limits of the universe are "arbitrary," its definition is predetermined, it is designated by an "abstract noun," and also, unfortunately, its interpretation varies. In 1949, the subordination of content

Table 8.1 Comparison of the Method of Samples and the Method of Signs

	Method of Samples	Method of Signs
Definition of universe	predefined	emergent
Limits of universe	arbitrary	empirical
Designation of universe	usually an abstract noun	behavioral in terms of probability
Interpretation of terminology	varies to a greater or lesser degree with different workers	comparatively uniform

SOURCE: Goodenough (1949, p. 100).

validity to construct validity was already established, though not in such words. Goodenough also perceived that the boundary between sample and sign is permeable: If we deal with inferences within the same universe, the behavior is both sample and sign (see also Messick, 1981a). The method of signs would function only to the extent that inferences are made from a sample of behavior from one universe to behavior from another. In this case, the inference can be made either on the basis of "blind empiricism" (which was fairly common in the tasks for prediction some decades ago) or on the basis of conceptual support—and is therefore tied to the problems of construct validation. Six years after the publication of Goodenough's book, the concept of nomological network (Cronbach & Meehl, 1955) shed light on this matter.

Conclusion

Issues of content validation have evolved in psychometric thought, but some behavioral assessors seem to ignore that evolution. Content validity does not hold up by itself; both the ideas at its base, "representative sample" and "universe of responses" (or even "universe of stimuli"), need conceptual support. For this reason, problems of content validation are now generally considered as problems of construct validation. This replacement within construct validity should not make us forget the requirements of concreteness and objectivity that fueled the concept of content validity and that, hence, served to develop and exploit its possibilities.

This chapter has noted some observations about the distinction, originally made by Goodenough (1949), between the sample approach and the sign approach. A careful reading of Goodenough shows that the interpretation of this distinction made by Goldfried and Kent (1972), and by many others after them, is inadequate. The Goldfried-Kent formulation is probably based on Mischel (1968) rather than Goodenough. For Goodenough, the sign approach has to do with an exclusively empirical orientation to predictive validity and the sample approach with a theoretical orientation to the same, where the scientific concepts (or constructs) play an essential role. Along a somewhat different line than that developed by behavioral assessors, Goodenough foretold the subordination of content validity to construct validity, anticipating the view that would become dominant in the scientific community.

Notes

1. A strong controversy about the status of content validity has indeed taken place (see, e.g., Morales, 1988). After Messick's (1989) arguments, however, this controversy should be obviated. He also reminds us that placing the problems of content validation within construct validation by no means reduces their importance.

2. From this new perspective, the question regarding representativeness of stimuli and representativeness of responses, in reality, moves to a second plane, at the same time that both begin to appear inseparable. It would be erroneous to defend a perspective on the constructs that disregards either of the two aspects, for the simple reason that a behavioral construct must, by definition, involve both.

3. Fernández-Ballesteros (1983b) later recognizes another, even higher, level of inference in which signs and constructs make up a complete theory.

9

CONSTRUCT VALIDITY

It is now time to take up construct validity, a concept introduced in the very first version of the APA *Standards*. If we follow the remarks of Wittenborn in his 1957 review, and Loevinger in her 1959 review, the concept has been well received and its use has expanded rapidly. It is certain, however, that this concept frequently has been neglected and even misunderstood. "It is somewhat paradoxical," Hogan and Nicholson (1988) write, "that, after all the recent serious discussion of personality measurement, many psychologists seem unaware of the literature on construct validity and what it means for evaluating new personality measures" (p. 624). Therefore, I must comment on this topic at some length.

The fundamental publication on the subject, "Construct Validity in Psychological Tests," by Cronbach and Meehl (1955), actually contains, in its final summary, the different aspects and directions through which construct validity has developed. Rewording at times to facilitate the explanation, I will focus this discussion on the 10 points made in that summary.

1. First is the issue of definition. What does *construct validity* mean? The concept of validity has been dealt with in Chapter 6, but the term

construct remains to be considered. Even within the literature on validity, *construct* is not used in a singular way. For Cronbach and Quirk (1976), "a construct is a category created in order to organize experience into general statements having the form of laws" (p. 170). A very similar definition is given in the 1974 *Standards*: "A psychological construct is an idea developed or 'constructed' as a work of informed, scientific imagination; that is, it is a theoretical idea developed to explain and to organize some aspects of existing knowledge" (APA, AERA, & NCME, 1974, p. 29). On the other hand, Cronbach and Quirk speak of some constructs as referring to "internal processes" and as a "postulated attribute of people, assumed to be reflected in test performance" (Cronbach & Meehl, 1955, p. 283). Similarly, the 1985 *Standards* speak of a "psychological characteristic."

Now we can see two possible aspects: one purely epistemological, without substantialist pretensions, making the concept an instrument of knowledge; and another that implies transcendent reality for the construct, thus placing it, so to speak, within the subject. I will return to this matter below; now my interest is in emphasizing, together with Messick (1981a), that the developers of the concept of construct validity side with the first alternative. Construct is spoken of to emphasize its "constructed" character. Thus "concepts such as 'anxiety' and 'ability' are constructs (*'constructs'*), that is, terms that attempt to describe how actions or thoughts are organized" (Cronbach, 1984a, p. 45); a construct "is a theoretical concept derived from research and other experience that has been constructed to explain observable behavior patterns. When test scores are interpreted by using a construct, the scores are placed in a conceptual framework" (AERA, APA, & NCME, 1985, p. 90). This primarily concerns a problem of organizing experience: "Whenever one classifies situations, persons, or responses, he uses *constructs*. . . . Constructs for interpreting tests usually have been identified with a class of responses" (Cronbach, 1971, p. 462).

Then why speak about constructs and not about *concepts*? Cronbach (1971) attempts to clarify the distinction: "The term *concepts* might be used rather than *constructs,* but the latter term emphasizes that categories are deliberate creations chosen to organize experience into general law-like statements" (p. 462). A construct thus is a concept within a scientific framework (theoretical, as well as methodological and applied). Although the high requirements sometimes make it difficult to speak about constructs (e.g., Nunnally & Durham, 1975), it is agreed that, within that framework, *concept* and *construct* refer to the same thing (Freeman, 1965; Gómez Benito, 1986; Kerlinger, 1973). Therefore, the expression *conceptual validity* was, at some point, a synonym of *construct validity* (Drenth, 1969; Thorndike & Hagen, 1970), and Cattell cogently suggested, in 1964, that the expression *conceptual validity* is preferable to *construct validity* (see also Morales, 1988). If *concept* rather than *construct* had been used from the start, many misunderstandings could have been avoided.

Defining construct validity requires no more than applying the idea of validity. We can adopt Messick's (1975) definition:

> I think that any brief discussion of the meaning of a measure should center on the concept of validity and specifically, on the concept of construct validity, for that is the evidential basis for inferring a measure's meaning. Construct validation is the process of marshaling evidence in the form of theoretically relevant empirical relations to support the inference that an observed response consistency has a particular meaning. (p. 955)

Also, "construct validity is concerned with the psychological qualities contributing to a test score" (Cronbach & Quirk, 1976, p. 169); and "construct validity is concerned with understanding the underlying dimensions or attributes being measured through any test or observation process" (Schoenfeldt, 1984, p. 65), with the condition that "psychological qualities" are not reified and that "underlying attribute" need not be understood in the perspective of what has come to be known as an "attribute model" (e.g., Fernández-Ballesteros, 1980). In a *methodological* perspective, it is sufficient to understand "some particular feature of objects" as the definition of attribute, in order to emphasize the fact that "strictly speaking, one does not measure objects—one measures their attributes" (Nunnally, 1978, p. 7). The concept of construct validity originates in a metascientific theory with a neopositivist character (Cronbach & Quirk, 1976; Meehl, 1978) that is far from the substantialist theories that could support the "attribute model." Guion (1974) presents constructs as a general problem of psychology when he asserts that it is the case "that nearly every branch of psychology entertains problems involving the creation of scientific or technological constructs, that measures are and must be derived for such constructs, and that the ultimate worth of the enterprise does in fact depend on the validity of inferences drawn from such measurement" (p. 295).

2. Many authors emphasize the structural character of constructs: They would deal with entities supposedly static, "components of" and the like, assessed by descriptive procedures of morphological analysis. Such writers consider the procedures of factor analysis to be the fundamental methodological techniques of construct validation. However, to the extent that a construct is used to explain a subject's response to the assessment instruments, construct validation also deals with—perhaps above all—psychological *processes* (e.g., Anastasi, 1988; Cronbach & Quirk, 1976; Messick, 1975). Cronbach (1984a) is especially clear on the matter: "Sooner or later every

tester has to go behind the experience table and behind the test content, to say what processes seem to account for the response observed" (p. 133). To understand, as well as to intervene, he adds in a 1989 paper, we need "process constructs"; or, in Messick's (1988) words, "Inferences regarding processes require construct-related evidence" (p. 38). Kagan (1988) goes precisely into the processes involved in order to decide how many and which constructs to use.

3. From early days, people have attempted to analyze construct validity into components. For example, as noted in Chapter 5, Loevinger (1957; see also Messick, 1989; Wiggins, 1973) spoke of "substantive validity," "structural validity," and "external validity." The first concerns the specification of the construct, and the last two, the determination of its relationships. In 1960, Campbell distinguished "two types of construct validity: The first of these can appropriately be given the old-fashioned name [!] *trait validity*"; the second "could be called *nomological validity* and would represent the very important and novel emphasis of Cronbach and Meehl on the possibility of validating tests by using the scores from a test as interpretations of a certain term in a formal theoretical network" (p. 547; see also Embretson, 1983, who uses "construct representation" instead of "trait validity").

As has already been pointed out, Cronbach and Meehl (1955) understand constructs as essentially involved in a network of both theoretical and empirical relationships: "The statements connecting constructs with each other, and observable indicators with constructs, constitute a nomological network (*nomological* meaning law-like)" (Cronbach, 1971, p. 476). "The phrase *nomological network* . . . designate[s] the system of law-like relationships conjectured to hold between theoretical entities . . . and between theoretical entities and their observable indicators," comments Meehl (1978, p. 812). He clarifies that the term *nomological* is, in a strict sense, inappropriate; rarely, or never, in most of psychology, does one work at a level of laws or of deterministic relationships between variables. The term most often concerns probabilistic kinds of relationships that form "stochastological" rather than nomological networks. But this "ugly neologism" (as he puts it) has not prospered. Following this same line, Messick (1989) considers nomological networks to be a rather advanced level of validation and suggests that they be no longer seen "as a requirement or defining feature of construct validation" (p. 23). The reader should keep Meehl's as well as Messick's remarks in mind—to which I will return below—although I will continue using the original expression.

4. In relation to both construct definition and the determination of its nomological network is what Campbell and Fiske (1959) call "convergent and discriminant validity." In the words of Messick (1975):

Construct validity has two major requirements. One is *convergent* evidence, by which it is demonstrated that the measure in question is substantially related to other measures of the same construct and to other variables that it should relate to on theoretical grounds. Equally important, however, is *discriminant* evidence, whereby it is shown that the measure is not related unduly to indicators of other distinct constructs. (p. 956; see also Messick, 1980)

The discriminant aspect, which has progressively gained importance, is viewed by Cronbach (1971) as "an echo of the general methodological principle of parsimony, which states that different scientific names should not be applied to the same thing or the same construct" (p. 467). He finds the functional aspects of constructs more interesting than the structural when making a decision about fusing two of them; it may be appropriate, he says, to retain two highly correlated constructs if their behavior with respect to other variables differs in any important way (see also Cronbach, 1989). The physical sciences often retain highly correlated constructs such as weight and mass or atomic number and atomic weight (Cronbach, 1971).

It is well known that Campbell and Fiske have proposed a strategy to analyze the convergent and discriminant power of constructs and indicators: the "multitrait-multimethod matrix." Its acceptance has not been as general as that of the concepts that inspired it. There is also no agreement regarding how often it is used: Jackson and Paunonen (1980) find it to be rather rare, whereas Schoenfeldt (1984) notes increasing use. The most important questions, however, impinge here on the relation between method and construct, which we will touch upon further on.

5. If Campbell and Fiske's concepts of convergent and discriminant validity have become a good summary of the way to analyze the nomological network, it must not be forgotten that their original idea (the direct inspiration of the multitrait-multimethod matrix) was to break down the observed covariances. They argued that the construct should be independent of any specific method through which it is evaluated, and proposed the intermethod convergence as proof of such independence.

Many authors are forthrightly against this requirement. McClelland (1981) writes that "Campbell and Fiske . . . were wrong in arguing that theory requires . . . consistencies across methods of measurement" (p. 93; see also the critical remarks of Kroger, 1968; Ozer, 1989). Whether that is accepted or not, Campbell and Fiske deserve credit for emphasizing the impact of method variance throughout the assessment process. Recently, Fiske (1987) has described threats to construct validation that come from method effects.

Method and construct cannot be considered completely separate things. An appropriate definition of a construct contains a methodological perspective that tells us something about the strategies by which it must be measured:

> The investigation of construct validity must study a construct-operation unit, not a construct and some casually selected procedure for its measurement. The specific measuring procedure must be involved integrally in the total conceptual formulation being subjected to empirical test. . . . The empirical investigation of construct validity assesses the validity of the integration of the method with the construct, that is, the validity of that form of the construct which is measured by the test. Hence, the empirical validation of a personality construct is possible, in principle, provided the investigation employs a measuring procedure which has been explicitly linked to the construct and its conceptual context. (Fiske, 1973, pp. 89, 92)

In their 1955 article, Cronbach and Meehl had already pointed out that the studies of construct validation estimate the validity of both the construct and the instrument. The first *Standards* are very clear in this respect: "One tends to ask regarding construct validity just what is being validated—the test or the underlying hypothesis? the answer is, *both,* simultaneously" (APA, 1954, p. 15). Cronbach (1984a) readdresses this idea: "Validity of test and validity of construct are inseparable. When a new test is considered for a well-accepted construct, the test is at risk more than the construct. Still, the evidence could compel revision of the construct. A particularly notable example is the abandonment of traditional ideas of 'feeblemindedness' " (p. 151).

Despite the intimate relation of construct and method, it is advisable that a construct be connected with more than one specific method. Lacking that richness, it is caught in a vicious circle; the construct is then isolated and not connected to a nomological network. Nunnally and Durham (1975) convincingly argue this point. Therefore, Cronbach (1984a) varies McClelland's criticism quoted above and sees an effective use in the strategy proposed by Campbell and Fiske (see also Cronbach, 1989). He was explicit in 1971 that "the criterion is an indicator of a construct that, like most powerful constructs, should transcend any particular method of observation" (p. 488).

6. Now, what is the status of constructs within science? First, *constructs and construct validation are inseparably linked to empirical evidence.* Hence it would be entirely inappropriate to speak of "theoretical validity" and "empirical validity" as if one opposed or excluded the other. From their beginnings, the statements with respect to construct validity insist on this, as well as provide an increasingly varied range of both correlational and experimental or manipulative empirical validation procedures. Cronbach and Quirk (1976), pointing out that "the justification of a construct is

strengthened when the construct predicts more and more diverse observations," go on to say: "The evidence must be made public so that other scientists may criticize and offer alternative interpretations. Nonpublic evidence which refers to something 'observed by the writer in many clinical cases' is worthless as evidence because refutation of the researcher's report is impossible (Cronbach & Meehl, 1955)" (p. 171).

More concretely, the referents of psychological constructs are behavioral; they have a clearer and more promising future if they are limited to the "realm of behavior" (Fiske, 1979), and the closer they are to these characteristics, the better. Tenopyr (1977) offers, "My general advice is, 'If you want to use inferences about test construction to justify inferences about test scores, stay with simple, well-defined constructs with easily observable manifestations' " (p. 54). This same approach can also be seen in Fiske (1987) and in Nunnally and Durham (1975), among others.

A construct is not, however, reducible to its empirical referents. This point also has been clear from the beginning. Too much is lost in an attempt to reduce a construct to an operational definition or to identify the construct with an intervening variable—although this is proposed by some authors (e.g., Goldfried, 1977; Goldfried & Linehan, 1977; Linehan, 1980). Messick (1975) points out that

> the measure is not equated with the construct nor considered to define the construct, in contrast to strict operationism in which each construct is defined in terms of a narrowly specified set of operations that becomes its single empirical referent. Rather, a construct is defined by a network of relations that are tied to observables and hence are empirically testable. (p. 955; see also Messick, 1989)

Cronbach and Quirk (1976) remind us of the origin and meaning of this position:

> [The] insistence upon operational definitions would force thinking into a rigid mold and force the abandonment of many useful concepts. In developing the idea of construct validation, Cronbach and Meehl (1955) joined the philosophers of science who dissent from a strict operationalism in which every term is defined by one, and only one, set of operations. When there are many response variables, they argued, it is mandatory to subsume them under constructs, since otherwise there must be a separate set of laws for every measure of outcome. (p. 170)

Philosophers of science seem to agree with this. In 1978, Meehl wrote with a certain irony, "I cannot name a single logician or a philosopher (or historian) of science who today defends strict operationism in the sense that some psychologists claim to believe in it" (p. 815). The growing acceptance attained by Wittgenstein's notion of "prototype," which decries reduction to the operational, is noted by Rorer and Widiger (1983), who add: "Do you suppose that Cronbach and Meehl smiled just a little bit when they read [about this]? Now that hypothetical constructs have been renamed, maybe research on them will become not only acceptable but respectable" (p. 457).

Concepts inserted in scientific theories retain a significant reserve that cannot be exhausted in an operationalization. Because of this, Hogan and Nicholson (1988) call the constructs "open concepts," taking this expression from Pap (quoted by Messick, 1989, p. 17). "Technically speaking," writes Messick (1981b), "once we depart from a strict behavioral description . . . and proceed to speak of skill . . . we invoke a construct having surplus meaning that requires additional empirical grounding" (p. 11). This "surplus" is then what moves research and scientific progress: "A construct cannot be reduced to observables since it contains 'surplus meaning.' This surplus meaning contains the potential for future scientific development and is 'an indispensable part of theory for those who are concerned with the progress of scientific knowledge' (Caws, 1965, p. 58)" (Cronbach & Quirk, 1976, p. 171). In turn, that same characteristic is the basis of a potential for its *usefulness* (Rorer & Widiger, 1983), opening possible horizons for explanation and prediction (Drenth, 1969; Silva, 1982).

A construct has an exclusively epistemological status. This must be made perfectly clear. Sometimes expressions are ambiguous and should be seen in light of a concrete historic moment. However, the developers of the theory for construct validation have been coherent in that "they ascribe only systematic existence . . . and are seemingly reluctant to attribute reality to either the constructs or their referents, the postulated attributes or traits" (Messick, 1981a, p. 579). Without doubt, this author has the words of Loevinger (1957) in mind:

> Traits exist in people; constructs . . . exist in the minds and magazines of psychologists. . . . It is true that psychologists never know traits directly but only through the glass of their constructs, but the data to be judged are manifestations of traits, not manifestations of constructs. Cronbach and Meehl and their colleagues on the APA committee appear reluctant to assign reality status to constructs or traits. (p. 642)

The above-cited article by Messick (1981a) on "constructs and their vicissitudes" is an excellent and systematic review of the matter that concerns us now (see also Messick, 1989). Remember that, with regard to the scientific status of constructs and traits, authors can take or, at least, have taken three different postures. One is the realist point of view; another, the logical-constructivist; and a third, the constructivist-realist. If one reads Messick's article carefully, one can see that all that involves realism refers to traits, and not to constructs. Thus, from the second point of view, which is most characteristic of psychometric theory, the trait has no place (see Figure 2 in the article cited), whereas from the realist point of view, it is the construct that does not appear (see Figure 1). Constructs, remember, have no other role than that of concepts and their relations within scientific theory:

> From this logical-constructivist standpoint the main function of constructs is to provide inductive summaries of observed relationships as a basis for elaborating networks of theoretical laws (Beck, 1950; Cronbach & Meehl, 1955). Constructs thus provide organized interpretations of observed behaviors, as well as a means of predicting previously unobserved behavioral consistencies from the theoretical implications of the nomological network. (Messick, 1981a, p. 580)

Nunnally and Durham (1975) also express this point of view in a pure way, so to speak, when they remind us that "the words that scientists use to denote constructs, for example, 'anxiety' and 'intelligence', have no real counterparts in the world of observables; they are only heuristic devices for exploring observables" (p. 307). Finally, Binning and Barrett (1989) summarize this issue in a recent work:

> Psychological *constructs* are labels for clusters of covarying behaviors. . . . Putting aside the perennial debate on the objective existence of psychological traits and psychologist's constructs (Cronbach & Meehl, 1955; Kane, 1982; Loevinger, 1957; Messick, 1981[a]; Nunnally, 1978), viewed pragmatically, a construct is merely a hypothesis about which behaviors will reliably covary. . . . In other words, psychologists hypothesize both (a) whether certain behaviors will covary and (b) whether the clusters of covarying behaviors (constructs) tend to covary in meaningful ways. In this general sense, the terms *construct validation* and *theory development* imply the same basic process. (p. 479)

We will come back to this last point later on.

Although one may not agree with the strictly nominalist point of view that statements such as these may contain, it seems to me more important nowadays to guard against the realistic temptation than against the nominalist; better said, it is more important to guard against the *confusion* between constructs and reality or proposed entities that—from an implicitly substantialist or essentialist conception—would underlie what is observable. The latter is found in some conceptions of personality and traits and, surely, as an implicit assumption of classical test theory. But it is abusive and erroneous to attribute a realist conception to the theory of psychological constructs. Constructs are not "behind" behavior but rather "in front of it," between the individual's responses and the scientist who attempts to understand them, and with that, to predict and modify them if necessary. It may be said that they are, along the lines of Kelly (1955) and using Jones and Nisbett's (1972) expression, "in the eyes of the beholder." "A construct is an intellectual device by means of which one *construes* events. It is a means of organizing experience into categories. A culture forms a category when it is observed that certain things have similar causes, consequences, or correlates" (Cronbach, 1971, p. 464).

We know that Jones and Nisbett's expression, cited above, is applied to an attempt to reformulate the concept of trait in which Mischel has had a prominent role since the time of his 1968 book, in which he unfortunately speaks of "trait or construct validity." It is also possible that the trait may have a similar status to the construct or that there is a trait-construct isomorphism, as the constructivist-realist focus presented by Messick (1981a) alleges. I do not enter here into the issue of the concept, scientific status, and current importance of traits; I only insist that trait must not be confused with construct, which does seem to have a clear status. I believe it is an error to set different "construct levels" depending on whether they are more or less "external" or "internal," as Fiske (1987) does. What "construct level" concerns is not entities that are more or less external or internal but rather *different levels of abstraction* (e.g., Morales, 1988; Nunnally, 1978) and from there, an explanatory and predictive claim more or less free-ranging. We previously saw a definite tendency toward the concretion and "regionalization," so to speak, of constructs, far from the excessive claims of many classical psychological theories. Nevertheless, there is no possible concretion level, in science, that exempts us from resorting to constructs. In this respect, Cronbach (1988) is graphic when he writes, "Questions of construct validity become pertinent the moment a finding is put into words" (p. 13).

Constructs are proposed not only to benefit theory but to improve prediction. Loevinger (1957, 1959) was surely the person who explained this idea most clearly: "Predictive validation construed as a program of test construction invariably means maximizing prediction of a single criterion. . . . Construct validation implies a program for simultaneous maximization of as many predictions as possible" (Loevinger, 1959, p. 289). In her 1957 article, Loevinger notes the unsatisfactory findings in cross-validation of tests lacking theoretical bases. Theoretical support is needed to approach transsituational prediction, an idea that Meehl (1959/1973a) explicitly supported (see also Cattell, 1964; Nunnally, 1978; Paunonen, 1984). (In a different context, Cook & Campbell, 1979, likewise see construct validity as a requirement in generalization.)

The value of a construct is judged by its usefulness. This is one of the consequences of what has been said in the two previous points and, more specifically, of the concept of construct itself. Cronbach (1971) points out that "the subsequent piling up of confirmations can establish enormous confidence in the usefulness of a construct and its indicators. Note the reference to *usefulness,* not to *truth*" (p. 477). "There is no implication that the constructs reflect existential reality but, rather, instrumental utility," adds Messick (1989, p. 29). And Nunnally and Durham (1975) state: "The evidence obtained is not so much proof of the *truth* of the theories as it is proof of their *usefulness* as guides to empirical reality. Call it the 'measurement' and 'validation' of constructs if you like" (pp. 308-309; see also Nunnally, 1978). Naturally, one can speak of truth, but on the condition that its metaphysical claims be left outside. Constructs and especially construct validation appeared to improve the explanatory and predictive power of certain scientific interpretations of observed behavior and still seems fitting to keep their original meaning.

7. In previous chapters, criterion-oriented validity and content validity were integrated into the framework of construct validity. The general idea is well expressed by Glass (1986):

> Measurements have meanings, and they permit or obstruct thinking to various degrees. The process by which measurements are taken, as well as the ideas that give rise to the measurements, are only judged in accord with how both—ideas and measurements—lead toward greater understanding. The relationship is reciprocal: constructs and observations, meanings and methods. The message is Cronbach and Meehl's. (p. 13)

Construct validity has become the core of a hierarchical and unifying view of validity. Loevinger's (1957) statement is a milestone in the theory of validity: "Since predictive, concurrent and content validities are all essentially ad hoc, construct validity is the whole of validity from a scientific point of view" (p. 636). Messick (1981) adds:

> In the 25 years since these words were published, it has become increasingly clear that this seemingly radical doctrine is in actuality a central principle of educational and psychological measurement and that, if anything, it does not go far enough in stressing the fundamental role of construct validity—not just for scientific measurement but for applied measurement as well (Cronbach, 1971; Guion, 1976; Messick, 1975, 1980). (p. 9; see also Messick, 1988, 1989)

Thus *"all measurement should be construct-referenced"* (Messick, 1975, p. 957); *"all* validity is at its base some form of construct validity. . . . it is the basic meaning of validity" (Guion, 1977, p. 410). Quoting Guion's comment on the "trinitarian" conception of validity (see Chapter 6), Angoff (1988) writes humorously: "It may be said that the more recent view, in which construct validity comprises all of validity, holds that these three types [content validity, criterion-related validity, construct validity] are now to be regarded in a monotheistic mode as the three aspects of a unitary psychometric divinity" (p. 25). We can now understand Messick's (1980) succinct explanation perfectly:

> Construct validity is indeed the unifying concept of validity that integrates criterion and content considerations into a common framework for testing rational hypotheses about theoretically relevant relationships. The bridge or unifying theme that permits this integration is the meaningfulness or interpretability of the test scores, which is the goal of the construct validation process. This construct meaning provides a rational basis both for hypothesizing predictive relationships and for judging content relevance and representativeness. (p. 1015)

Anastasi (1986) has this to say:

> What has come to be designated construct validity is actually a comprehensive approach that includes the other recognized validation procedures—and much more besides. The point has been made repeatedly; in the test standards (from the first, 1954 version to the latest), in textbooks, symposium papers, and journal articles. . . . Content analyses and correlations with external criteria fit into particular stages in the process of construct validation, that is, in the process of both determining and demonstrating what a test measures. Certain procedures may be singled out for special emphasis in order to answer specific practical questions. But constructs are always involved, in both the questions and the answers, even though we may not be aware of it. (p. 4)

For Cronbach (1980), "All validation is one, and in a sense all is construct validation" (p. 99). Elsewhere, he says:

> It might appear that criterion validation is for aptitude tests, content validation for educational tests, and construct validation for personality tests, but that generalization is false. . . . The end goal of validation is explanation and understanding. Therefore, the profession is coming around to the view that *all* validation is construct validation. . . . Content- and criterion-based arguments develop parts of the story. (Cronbach, 1984a, p. 126)

Ideas such as these are now part of the psychometric thought of Western Europe (e.g., Baumann, 1981; Gómez Benito, 1986), and a very similar direction is found in Eastern Europe (e.g., Witzlack, 1974).

8. There is no limit to the strategies, procedures, instruments, and types of data potentially useful in construct validation. The 1974 *Standards* grasp this idea with complete clarity: "To evaluate construct validity, all knowledge regarding validity is relevant" (APA, AERA, & NCME, 1974, p. 26). This idea is taken up again by Anastasi (1986, p. 12), among others, when she writes that "all validation procedures contribute to construct validation and can be subsumed under it," which is in turn expanded upon by other authors (e.g., Cronbach, 1971; Fiske, 1971; Frederiksen, 1986). Thus "practically all psychometric procedures are involved, in one way or another, in the possible and complementary techniques of their construct validation" (Gómez Benito, 1986, p. 27; see also Anastasi, 1988; Angoff, 1988; Messick, 1988, 1989). Nor is the approach restricted to the psychometric; there is use to be made of other empirical methods, including the experimental, and there is place for logical or theoretical analysis (Cronbach, 1971).

9. "Construct validity . . . cannot be expressed in a single coefficient" (Angoff, 1988, p. 26) and not even in the form of a lot of numerical data. Construct validity must be evaluated from the whole of the investigation based on the instrument-construct dyad: "Statements about construct validity may use various statistics to support interpretations of the test, but there is no mathematical index of construct validity. Construct validity is an integrative interpretation of evidence" (Cronbach & Quirk, 1976, p. 170).

Nor does it concern a single exploration, but rather an accumulation of information: "Evidence of construct validity is not found in a single study; rather, judgments of construct validity are based upon an accumulation of research results" (APA, AERA, & NCME, 1974, p. 30). Anastasi (1986) writes: "Construct validation is indeed a never-ending process" (p. 4; see also Angoff, 1988; Franzen, 1989; Morales, 1988; Rust & Golombok, 1989). "A test score has an endless list of implications, and one cannot validate the entire list. Construct validation is therefore never complete. Construct validation is best seen as an ever-extending inquiry into the processes that produce a high or low test score and into the other effects of those processes" (Cronbach, 1971, p. 452).

10. A most important remark by Cronbach and Meehl (1955) is that "the investigation of a test's construct validity is not essentially different from the general scientific procedures for developing and confirming theories" (p. 301).

With good reason, construct validity has been translated into Spanish as "validez de hipótesis de trabajo" ("working hypothesis validity"; see the translation of Alvarez Villar in Cronbach, 1972). Cronbach and Quirk (1976) tell us that "construct validators investigate hypotheses about the processes . . . such processes cannot be observed directly, but controlled observations of behavior can evaluate the reasonableness of the hypotheses" (p. 170). It is because of this that "the most serious criticism to be made of programs of construct validation is that some of them are haphazard accumulations of data rather than genuine efforts at scientific reasoning" (Cronbach, 1971, p. 483). Messick (1975) expresses the most global idea in writing that "test validation in the construct framework is integrated with hypothesis testing and with all of the philosophical and empirical means by which scientific theories are evaluated" (p. 956; see also García Ramos, 1986; Messick, 1988). Cronbach (1984a) connects us with remarks from previous points:

> Explaining test scores is much like any scientific reasoning—a back-and-forth exchange between curiosity, speculation, collection of evidence, and critical review of possible interpretations of the evidence. . . . This lengthy—indeed, endless—process of revising hypotheses is referred to succinctly as construct validation. . . . For such a free-ranging program of analysis there is no simple or ideal design. (pp. 133-134)

Along this line, Franzen (1989) underlines that "there are several common ways to investigate the construct validity of a test. The most basic research method is *theory testing*" (p. 45; emphasis added). Hogan and Nicholson (1988) put the emphasis on these ideas to summarize the concept of construct validity in three points: (a) "All validity is construct validity," (b) "the process of test validation is hypothesis testing," and (c) "measurement-based research is formally identical with any other type of legitimate scientific inquiry" (p. 621; see also Cole & Moss, 1989).

The above, joined with the context of logical positivism in which it has developed, insists that the attempts of *falsification* are important (in Popper's sense) and advises against the dominant tendency toward a "confirmationist" investigation (Cronbach, 1989). "Validating an interpretation using a construct," Cronbach told us in 1971, "investigates the effect of each disturbing influence pointed out by the counterhypotheses" (p. 464). "Construct validation consists of an attempt to falsify a proposed interpretation. The evaluator identifies plausible rival hypotheses and looks for evidence that would support them, hoping not to find it" (Cronbach, 1984b, p. 701). Messick (1975) helps us round off the idea:

> Construct validation could proceed by methodically attempting to verify in turn a variety of derivations from the theoretical network, but it is more efficient to direct attention from the outset to vulnerabilities in the theory by formulating *counterhypotheses,* or plausible alternative interpretations of the

observed consistencies. If repeated challenges from a variety of plausible rival hypotheses can be systematically discounted, then the original interpretation becomes more firmly grounded (Chamberlain, 1965; Cronbach, 1971). (p. 956; see also Cronbach, 1984a; Messick, 1989)

Emphasis has shifted over the years. In the first publications, the purity of the process and the finished and formal character of the constructs were insisted upon. Cronbach (1989) was later to say that it could have been a tactical error to tie construct validation to the ideal deductive model, though the 1955 article with Meehl did emphasize the roughness and speculativeness of constructs. We really start with hypotheses and not with finished definitions. The finished definitions come later, out of reflection on the experience; better said, definitions are never finished (Cronbach, 1984a). Likewise, interpretations are more or less provisional, tied to "constructions" rather than to true theories (Cronbach, 1989; see also García Ramos, 1986; Messick, 1989; Tenopyr & Oeltjen, 1982). The interpretation must be basically contextual (e.g., Cole & Moss, 1989) and construct validation opens up new interpretations.

Construct validation is a fluid, creative process. . . . The interpretation has scientific aspects, but it often embodies policies and suggests practical actions. This complexity means that validation cannot be reduced to rules, and no interpretation can be considered the final word, established for all time. This has been a source of frustration and confusion. . . . Creating a long-lived theory is an unreasonably lofty aspiration for present day testers. . . . Test interpreters employ a scientific logic but—like engineers and physicians—they have to do the best they can now with comparatively primitive theory. (Cronbach, 1984a, p. 149; see also Cronbach, 1988; Morales, 1988)

This insistence that construct validation is tentative, unfinished, contextualized, although no less evolutionary and progressive—in the same sense in which a social science in a low advanced state of development may progress—is sound. The foremost criticisms made of construct validation, which fundamentally affect the status of the psychological science in that it is unable to fulfill the requirements that formalists call for, can be successfully overcome under that perspective (e.g., Bechtoldt, 1959/1967; Binning & Barrett, 1989; Lumsden, 1976; Meehl, 1959/1973a, 1979; Nunnally & Durham, 1975; Ozer, 1989; Taft, 1959/1971).

Construct Validity in Behavioral Assessment

After this necessary elaboration of construct validity, we can now turn to its place in behavioral assessment. Although the topic has deserved thorough consideration within an experimental approach to measurement of behavior (e.g., Alvira, Avia, Calvo, & Morales, 1979; Cook & Campbell,

1979), in behavioral assessment there is, without a doubt, a line contrary to the use of constructs and to validation related to them. Thus Hersen (1976), in his historical review, opposes "assessment of constructs" to "assessment of behaviors." This contrast goes back to Skinner. Fine (1969) quotes a revealing personal communication from Skinner: "I certainly do not believe there are psychological entities or events to be measured, and I'm quite content to proceed with the standard practices of the physical and biological sciences. So far as I can see there is no problem of measurement in psychology" (p. 533). A strange remark; in the physical and biological sciences there have always been problems of measurement, indicators are established, and interpretations via constructs are made. As for "psychological entities or events," it seems that presumed "intrapsychic entities" are referred to; on that I shall comment further on.

The work of Goldfried and Kent (1972) makes rejection of constructs and inferences mediated by constructs a fundamental theme. Taking up the schema of inference levels in personality assessment by Sundberg and Tyler (1962; see also Kleinmuntz, 1967), Goldfried and Kent distinguish between "traditional tests" and "behavioral tests." The former would employ constructs to mediate between observed responses in the tests and criterion responses; the latter would not. Responses observed in the behavioral test would constitute a sample of the criterion responses. Consequently, the validation question is one of content validity. This is, of course, consistent with the consideration of responses as samples of behavior rather than as signs of underlying intrapsychic entities.

Goldfried and Kent fall into some misunderstandings. In the first place, the persistent confusion between the conjectured underlying entities of an intrapsychic nature, usually know as "traits," and the hypothetical constructs appears. This is why I have attempted to clarify the status of constructs, which is epistemological and not ontological. In the second place, one supposes that the orientation toward samples of behavior is different, almost opposite, from the orientation toward constructs, that one can speak about content validation without touching construct validation. When Goldfried and Kent (1972) speak of "a population of criterion responses," one must ask what defines that population. When Goldfried and D'Zurilla (1969) speak of "response evaluation," one must ask just what it is that guides that evaluation, placing a different weight on distinct sectors, aspects, or components of the response. Conceptualizations certainly enter.

Let us consider an educational example, the germ of both content validity and "criterion-referenced measurement." If in claiming to assess knowledge of ancient history we put more weight on Greece and Rome than on other cultures—for example, Persia—does this not reflect what we understand by history and antiquity, that is, a certain perspective and a series of valuations? When we attempt to assess samples from "a population of criterion responses," the same thing occurs. It is naive to think that such "samplings" are not oriented by concepts, saturated in turn by valuations.

If Goldfried and Kent played an important role in stimulating antipathy toward constructs in behavioral assessment, then it was Cone who insistently sustained it. He began by correctly noting that "the thoroughness with which construct eradication takes place in behavioral assessment may determine the applicability of most classical [psychometric] procedures" (Cone, 1976, p. 2). Another paper points out, with evident disdain, that there are still even occasional suggestions that behavioral assessors be concerned with demonstrating construct validity (Cone & Hoier, 1986). In a 1981 article, Cone concludes by saying that "the assessment of behavior requires a radically different paradigm than the assessment of traits and hypothetical constructs" (1981b, p. 63). Unfortunately, his conception contains several errors.

Just as we saw in the last quotation, and continuing with a mistake that is usual not only in behavioral but also in psychometric tradition (e.g., Anastasi, 1988; APA, AERA, & NCME, 1974; Nunnally, 1978), Cone seems to identify or, at least, confound construct and trait. Likewise, a 1976 paper states that "constructs or traits" would be of no interest in behavioral assessment and that "types" of behavior are to be studied. Among such types, Cone cites "competence in heterosexual dating interaction," "interpersonal effectiveness," "heterosexual competence," "interpersonal competence," and "social anxiety." How can he, at the same time, say that "if . . . one speaks of the utility of multitrait-multimethod matrices simply in terms of the exposition of relationships among behaviors, avoiding the pejorative 'construct,' then they may be of use to behavioral assessors" (Cone, 1976)? Is not Cone, when speaking of "types" of behavior, speaking of "pejorative constructs"? The answer must be a very emphatic yes.

Cone's basic error seems to have been in seeing construct and behavior as opposites. Recently that opposition has weakened. "Construct validity," he writes,

> will be of no concern to behavioral assessors, in one sense since constructs are not the subject of interest, behavior is. In another sense, behavior can be seen as a construct itself, in which case the instrument will have construct validity to the extent that it "makes sense" in terms of the behavior as the client and the assessor understand it. (Cone, 1988, p. 59)

If "making sense" is not trivialized, that is exactly what construct validity is concerned with, at least as those who developed the concept understand it; with unraveling and giving meaning to observed behavior. Cone thinks it enough to move within the realms of face and content validity, but it is probable that much more is required.

With all this, Cone's attempt includes something positive, which he shares with his colleagues in behavioral assessment and with most psychological assessors of the recent psychometric tradition. It concerns trying to remain close to concrete and observable behavior. We have seen an example of how this desire is betrayed, but it should be noted that the intention is worthwhile and that it has given results of evident interest, as is the critical approach of the author toward the theory of the three response systems (e.g., Cone, 1977a, 1979; Cone & Hawkins, 1977b; Cone & Hoier, 1986). Among behavioral assessors, Nelson and Hayes (1986b), for example, support a withdrawal from constructs and an approach toward concrete behavior. The same remark is made by Fiske (1978, 1979), who clearly sees the behavioral approach to constructs as closely bonded to description and to low level of abstraction (if this is indeed so). The same tendency, as we have seen, is what led Goldfried and Linehan to propose that the expression *intervening variables* be used rather than constructs, even though I have questioned that proposal.

Constructs' concretion and approach to observable behavior is one thing; constructs' epistemological status as mediators of the explanation and prediction of behavior is another. Traits can be considered on a solely descriptive level, devoid of explanatory claims. For the constructs and nomological networks that develop them, that is impossible. When referring to constructs and nomological networks, one is referring to explanatory hypotheses of a lawful type. Naturally, we deal with an explanation in the sense that a law explains a certain behavior of things, not in the sense that the impact of one stone against another explains the movement of the latter, because it really does not explain anything. What explains, in this case, is the set of laws that relates mass, force, and direction under specific conditions.

In short, behind the rejection of constructs, there is a warning, in Cone, against the dangers of theorizing. "It may be that a period of atheoretical, unprejudiced, inductive empiricism may be necessary to the discovery of new relationships that will produce more satisfactory theory in the area" (Cone & Hawkins, 1977b, p. xix). If this sentence means a call to atheoreticism, it must be rejected (e.g., Chow, 1987; Manicas & Secord, 1983). But this does not seem to be the case. What that sentence seem to imply is a call, very similar to that of Cronbach in 1975, along the line of avoiding premature formalizations, of provisionality, contextualism, and opening up, which, as we have seen, characterizes the evolution that the concept of construct validity has had. Therefore, we must conclude that in behavioral assessment there is no convincing reason to reject such a concept.

Arguments against construct validity are lately fewer than claims for its necessity and convenience. This tendency has several origins. For example, social (paradigmatic) behaviorism claims a return to personality and a consideration of its basic components—the basic behavioral repertoires by Staats that were cited earlier, which contain allusions to assessment that are clearly similar to construct validation (e.g., Staats, 1975, 1986). In fact, when Messick (1981a) reviews the possible perspectives on constructs, social behaviorism is seen to be clearly reflected in the constructivist-realist position: "If the terms *trait* and *personality structure* are replaced . . . with terms like *response class* and *stimulus conditions,* then the diagram comes to represent the position of many social behaviorists" (p. 582; see also Messick, 1989). Evans (1986) writes, "It is obvious that behavioral assessment uses constructs and that no science of behavior or model of behavioral measurement could exist without so doing" (p. 135), and Haynes (1991, p. 144) adds: "Perhaps the most important dimension for evaluating an assessment instrument, but also a source of debate (Cone, 1988), is the degree to which it measures the construct it is intended to measure." It must not be forgotten that among questions related to the measurement of behavior, Skinner (1938) saw "the definition of a response as a class of events" (p. 58). Well, Messick (1988) is conclusive about this: "The notion of a . . . behavioral class is a construct. The notion is of a class of behaviors all of which change in the same or related ways as a function of stimulus contingencies or that share or are organized by common processes" (p. 39). With respect to this, it is likewise appropriate to remember some remarks made by Peterson in his 1968 book:

> The principal dangers in positing constructs are those of circularity and reification. But both can be avoided if the constructs are stated in such ways as to generate testable predictions and if these in fact are tested. Cronbach and Meehl (1955) have written persuasively to this point. . . .
>
> To be useful, statements about human behavior must always move from discrete accounts of singular events to general positions of some kind. Scientists and clinicians are always concerned with classes of events and classes of conditions which determine those events. The statements which result are probabilistic, not declaratively certain, and this holds for classes of strictly observable stimuli and responses as much as for covert events. . . . The only relevant question is a pragmatic one. Can useful behavioral propositions be arrived at more effectively and efficiently by introducing mediating constructs or by omitting them? For the kinds of events of concern in this book there is no clear answer at the present time.
>
> It is well to remember that the Behavioristic prohibition against constructs is a theoretical preference and no more. It is an opinion, not a law. It offers

a gain in objectivity at the possible risk of less than optimal generative power. The supposed gain in parsimony by which Radical Behaviorists justify their position rarely accrues and the tortured efforts to explain thought processes in strict S-R terms are usually ludicrous. There is little scientific profit in developing a complex chain of S-R propositions to explain events which can be much more simply accommodated by simple verbal inquiries and sensible inference of central events. (pp. 64-65)

The problem, is, however, more general. A while ago, Weiner (1972), among others, pointed to a danger of impoverished theory that seemed to be perceptible in the behaviorist approach to assessment: Many times it would have avoided studying deeply to understand prediction or control and change of behavior. It may be argued how effective the following has been, but it is worthwhile to draw attention to it: Explanatory hypotheses about processes that determine behavior are needed in assessment. Likewise, "let it be suggested that the critics read the literature more carefully, for when they weigh the results of studies rooted in solid conceptual design, they will find reason to lower their voices" (Weiner, 1972, p. 537). Years later, Kendall (1985) states that "the lack of a conceptual framework has hindered the advance of behavioral assessment" (p. 49), adding this lack to the sources of the behavioral assessor's disappointment of which Nelson (1983a) spoke. McFall (1986) relates this deficit of theory directly to constructs:

Many behaviorists regard hypothetical constructs as anathemas. This attitude is not typical of more advanced scientific disciplines, such as physics, with constructs like momentum and force, or biology, with constructs like symbiosis and evolution. There is no reason to assume that psychology cannot make progress by entertaining hypothetical constructs of its own. The key, of course, is whether our constructs increase our ability to predict and control, not whether they conform to our prejudices. (p. 6)

Problems of construct validation have been outlined, in behavioral assessment, in different scopes. We have more than once insisted that however much one works with very limited and operational definitions of target behaviors, a conceptualization is always there. Through reference to behavioral assessment, Cronbach (1984a) wrote that "the fineness of categories will depend on the purpose of an inquiry, but categories there must be" (p. 46; see also Messick, 1989), to which it is added that "the requirement for construct validation can be easily seen whenever behavioral categories are involved" (Hartmann et al., 1979, p. 13). This, aside from the fact that "behaviorists may measure fairly general traits" (Cronbach, 1984a, p. 46). When we read, "If one is interested in deviant or aggressive acts as they distinguish groups of referred and nonreferred children, no construct is necessarily implied" (Cone, 1982, p. 75), we should object forcefully. The construct "aggressiveness" is certainly implied! Haynes (1990, p. 428) states that "despite the strong emphasis on observables, inferential concepts are not alien to behavioral construct systems, and are frequently the focus of behavioral assessment efforts." In the 1984 review by Kendall, it can be seen that questions of this kind arise time and time again, as well as the need to explore nomological networks. This is noted in relation to social skills, social anxiety, hyperactivity, aggressiveness, self-control, and so on. In this same sense, we find an attempt at construct validation in the area of antisocial behavior—with insistence on the nomological vein—in a work by Patterson and Bank (1986). While dealing with the subject of aggressive behavior, Kanfer and Nay (1982) make some very pertinent comments:

> Assessors could argue exhaustively about the difference between aggressive behavior as a "sign" of a trait or merely a "sample" of the client's behavior. Regardless, this particular assessor's construction of aggressiveness is expressed as soon as the assessor makes predictions about family members that go beyond the specific occasion of assessment (e.g., how the family might behave when the assessor is not present). In summary, when a limited behavioral observation is used to describe a client as "aggressive," this implies that the assessor is satisfied that the person has shown a sufficient subset of behaviors that fit the *assessor's* construction of aggressiveness. (p. 388)

The same authors add a complementary observation: "The nature of the assessor's constructs also relates to selection of an evaluation strategy for the methods employed" (p. 388). As a matter of fact, we have seen, concerning the concept of construct, how this is indissolubly linked to particular measurement strategies (even though the definition should likewise go beyond any particular strategy). We now find this idea in an article on behavioral assessment: "There is another less obvious sense in which construct validation may be required in behavioral assessment. The observation of behavior is often so direct that it is easy to forget that every observation reflects the method used to make it, and thus every observation is actually a behavior/method unit" (Hartmann et al., 1979, p. 14). If we think, for example, about the three response systems and do the necessary testing of the assessment instruments with respect to each, we clearly see how much importance these considerations may obtain, as well as the aid that the psychometric developments with respect to construct validation may contribute in this specific area.

The need for constructs has become more pressing to the extent that behavioral assessment has broadened its field of action. The influence of the ecopsychological perspective has been decisive in this sense; it is sufficient to recall the compilation by Rogers-Warren and Warren (1977). On the one hand, that perspective concerns the need to "increase the range of environmental phenomena that they [the behavior analysts] seek to manipulate" (Wahler & Fox, 1981, p. 328). On the other hand, the ecopsychological approach involves increasing the analysis units regarding both the stimular vein and that of response. Barrios (1988) summarizes this tendency clearly:

> Traditionally, the number of phenomena that could serve as a legitimate treatment target has been limited to one. Tradition is not, however, as strong a force as it once was. Clusters of responses such as those denoting the diagnostic categories of the American Psychiatric Association (1980) are now seen by most as acceptable targets for behavioral treatments (Nelson & Barlow, 1981; Kazdin, 1983; Kratochwill, 1985; Nathan, 1981; Nelson & Hayes, 1981; Taylor, 1983) and by many as the most acceptable targets for behavioral treatments. (p. 11)

Barrios is decidedly partisan to a syndromatic approach, as contrasted with a symptomatic one, even though "both the syndrome and the symptom are constructions" (p. 19). (I would add that if reality is complex, then the symptomatic can involve a higher level of abstraction than the syndromatic.) It is from there, in any case, that we ought to guide ourselves, "by one's conceptualization of the problem space and one's definition of the problem" (Barrios, 1988, p. 11; see also Evans, 1986; Hayes & Nelson, 1986; Haynes, 1983, 1986; Hersen, 1988; Kazdin, 1985; Nelson, 1988; Nelson & Maser, 1988; Wahler & Fox, 1981).

The enlargement of the field of action proceeds in further directions: to consider a much broader temporal period than that traditionally recommended, in order to observe either mediating influences on behavior or mediating consequences of that behavior on the environment (e.g., Wahler & Fox, 1981); to consider interrelationships of responses that may have functional value and relevance in studies of the generalization of effects; and so forth.

Let us remember just one other way in which behavioral assessment has determinedly expanded: assessment strategies. Haynes (1983) speaks of the decided tendency toward a "broad-spectrum behavioral assessment," picking up a generalized conception. This is one of the principal meanings of "multiple operationalizations" that Shadish (1986) detected as frequent, which should not be abused yet has undoubted advantages. How could we forget Cone's (1976, 1978a, 1981a) repeated concern for a multimethod approach? Well, the necessary connection of such an approach to the problems of construct validity became clear upon explanation of the concept. Hayes and Nelson (1986) explicitly make this same remark. In summary, it seems appropriate to follow the advice of Barrios and Hartmann (1986): If behavioral assessment wants to be recognized and respected as a scientific discipline, *there must be a change in attitude that forments the systematization of the assessment process and that intelligently adopts many of the concepts and methods of psychometric assessment.* Among these, construct validity is first.

We still have not, however, arrived at the nucleus of what construct validation means in the perspective of behavioral assessment. Nelson and Hayes (1979b) took an important step in proposing what they call "conceptual validity." The questions brought up with regard to this are as follows: " 'Does this procedure or experiment increase our understanding of behavior?' That is, does the design of this procedure or experiment and its results enable us to support, extend, modify, or elaborate behavioral principles or assumptions?" (p. 11). In their 1981 article, they go back to this point: One speaks about conceptual validity when one asks why phenomena happen, for which "both thorough descriptions and experimental analyses of assessment issues" are required (Nelson & Hayes, 1981, p. 25). The process through which therapeutic effects are produced is set within a theoretical orientation of therapeutic research (Hayes et al., 1986, 1987).

The ideas included in Nelson and Hayes's conceptual validity help us understand what the fundamental role of construct validity is in behavioral assessment—which also corresponds, as we saw above, to its most characteristic meaning: *to be identified with what is strictly called functional analysis of behavior.* I noted this some years ago:

Constructs do have an important place and role. . . . What happens is that they do not have it [primarily] on the level of detection or assessment of behaviors, neither of its rates nor its concomitants. They play a role when, beyond the cluster of responses and circumstances, we postulate functional links and more precisely, we interpret these links in function with psychological processes which, no doubt, are constructs of a generally high degree of abstraction. If the covariation Behavior of a child crying-Behavior of the mother's approach is postulated as a functional link and is, more precisely, interpreted in function with an operant learning paradigm in such a way that we rename the child's behavior as operant crying and the mother's behavior as positive reinforcement, then we are working in relation to a conceptual system. These types of transformations, as we know, are essential in a functional analysis of behavior. It is precisely what allows us to arrive at the formulation of therapeutic models which are later transformed into concrete plans for treatment. (Silva, 1978, pp. 49-50)

Messick (1981a) refers to the most general framework of this remark when, from the perspective of construct validity, he uncovers the parallelism that exists between the functional analysis, which attempts to identify situational variables that elicit and support concrete behaviors, and the task analysis, which attempts to identify the characteristics of the task or job that elicit and support an adaptive performance. Barrios and Hartmann (1986) comment on how working at a construct level takes us beyond the correlational level of criterion-oriented validation by postulating causal relationships and hence hypotheses about agents that support behaviors and that it is necessary to explore more in depth. In turn, R. Jones (1983) calls attention to the essentially interpretive, theoretical character of all functional analyses and to how ignorance of this could lead to the elaboration of erroneous positions rather than to their correction. The following paragraphs clearly recall what Cronbach, Messick, and others have noted on the process of construct validation:

> The point here is that there is no single correct functional analysis of a particular case history or body of knowledge. Rather there are a number of possible formulations, some of which seem more probable than others on the basis of our knowledge of psychological processes and indeed of our particular perspective on mankind.
>
> A formulation in its strictest sense refers to a set of interlinking hypotheses. By this criterion a functional analysis is not an end but merely a means to an end. Functional analysis is an invaluable aid in setting up testable hypotheses. Where evidence cannot be found, however, adherence to any hypothesis should be seriously questioned and a revised functional analysis is required. (R. Jones, 1983, p. 238)

Functional analysis involves the preliminary collection of information (and with that, necessarily, conceptualization and categorization), the formulation of functional hypotheses (that is, the resource of learning paradigms that are credible working on the maintenance of the target behavior according to the information gathered), and also the experimental testing of such hypotheses. Thus functional analysis is nothing but a *process of construct validation.* Haynes and Wilson (1979) give this exact meaning to construct validation. The same idea is stated by Haynes (1986) when he speaks of "conceptual validation," an expression used now, surely, because of Nelson and Hayes's influence, and that, as we have seen, refers to what we are pointing out: the postulation and testing of functional links. On the other hand, Hawkins (1986) attempts to take importance away from "hypothetical constructs" and "validity inferences" in functional analysis, emphasizing the low level of abstraction in which they work. Yet, although this may be true—and on a functional level of behavior acquisition and change models it is, at least, debatable—we have seen that *the degree of abstraction is not the most important point in construct validation.* What is important is the process of hypothesis construction and testing. This idea is present when Hawkins (1986) himself writes that "in a functional analysis—a term used here to mean a conceptual analysis of functional relations between stimuli and responses, or between responses alone—behavior is described as embedded in functional relations" (p. 345; see also Turkat & Meyer, 1982).

In summary, inferences, concepts, and theoretical perspectives are found at different stages of behavioral assessment: "For assessment data to be helpful in formulating and evaluating the inferences on which the actions of therapy hinge, they must be interpreted. Contrary to popular belief, assessment data do not speak. Assessment data in and of themselves have no voice meaning" (Barrios, 1988, p. 26).

> Assessment data . . . do not and cannot perform many of the functions that many have mistakenly ascribed to them. Assessment data do not and cannot identify problem areas or determine controlling variables or select an intervention or evaluate an intervention (e.g., Nelson & Hayes, 1981). Assessment data can give rise to inferences, which in turn can give rise to decisions vis-à-vis identification of problem areas, determination of controlling variables, selection of an intervention, and evaluation of an intervention. (Barrios, 1988, p. 8)

Behavioral assessment must be conceived as a "cybernetic system" that links data with conceptualization and theory (Haynes, 1983). How could this not be related to construct validity and its own evolution? Even though construct validity

> was originally developed to permit an evaluation of certain theoretical ideas about individual personality characteristics, we believe that the behavioral assessor in certain important respects operates as a theorist, whether the assessment task involves preintervention assessment, assessment for purposes of clinical decision making, assessment of outcome, or assessment to describe or understand some phenomenon. (Kanfer & Nay, 1982, pp. 386-387)

Conclusion

This chapter has been longer than the rest for two reasons. The first is because the meaning and reach of construct validity tend not to be understood adequately by either psychometric or behavioral assessors. The second is because all that was previously said with respect to validity points to construct validity as the concept that both unifies and gives meaning. The concept of construct validity and its most important implications have been developed here, and the following list summarizes the 10 points made:

1. Constructs must be considered without any reifying pretension. *Construct* is synonymous with *scientific concept*, and construct validity is synonymous with conceptual validity or degree of appropriateness of conceptual or theoretical inferences made from assessment data.

2. Constructs must not be considered static. Above all, when we are dealing with "understanding in order to modify," constructs that refer to processes gain importance.

3. Constructs appear related, generally in a probabilistic way, to observable indicators and other constructs, constituting "nomological networks."

4. A classical way to explore both the definition of the construct and the nomological network into which it is inserted is provided by Campbell and Fiske's (1959) convergent and discriminant validation.

5. All construct validation refers to both the concept and the method involved. Nevertheless, it is highly advisable that a construct be measured by more than one assessment instrument.

6. The status of constructs in the scientific system can be summarized as follows: (a) Both constructs and construct validation are indisputably linked to empirical evidence; (b) a construct is not, however, reduced to its empirical referents—it always maintains a "surplus" meaning; (c) the construct has a fundamentally epistemological status—it is a means of knowledge, it is not "behind" the behavior but rather "in front of" it, between the behavior and the scientist studying it; (d) constructs are proposed with the goal of increasing prediction;and and (e) the value of a construct is judged by its usefulness.

7. Construct validity includes the concepts of criterion-oriented validity and content validity, at the same time involving the most current conceptions of validity. From a psychometric perspective, the concept of construct validity is identical to that of validity.

8. There is no limit to the potentially useful strategies, procedures, instruments, and types of data in construct validation.

9. Construct validity is not expressed in one or several coefficients; rather, it is judged in the light of all the information accumulated with respect to a proposed hypothesis. Moreover, no term can be given to the process of construct validation, to the extent that it can never be viewed as complete.

10. Construct validation essentially consists of the application of the process of scientific hypothesis formulation and testing in the field of psychological assessment (emphasizing the importance of falsification attempts). It is, however, not advisable to demand the degree of formalization required in more developed sciences or in basic research not pressured by practical requirements.

Within this perspective on construct validation, we come to two main consequences that can be enunciated perhaps most clearly with Nunnally's (1978) words:

> Scientists cannot do without constructs. Their theories are populated with them, and even in informal conversation scientists find it all but impossible to discuss their work without using words relating to constructs. It is important to keep in mind . . . that science is primarily concerned with developing measures of constructs and finding functional relations between measures of different constructs. (p. 97)

And further:

> The logical status of constructs in psychology concerning individual differences is the same as that for constructs concerning the results of controlled experiments. Thus, whereas the construct of intelligence is discussed more frequently with respect to studies of individual differences and the construct of habit strength is discussed more frequently with respect to controlled experiments, problems of construct validity are essentially the same for both. (p. 98)

In behavioral assessment there is, at least originally, a clear rejection of constructs and hence of the validation related to them. We have, however, been able to see that an adequate conceptualization of construct validity counteracts the criticisms from behavioral assessment—in particular, those that come from a reifying or substantialist viewpoint of constructs. On the other hand, the most recent evolution of behavioral assessment involves, in several ways, a greater need for this perspective on validity (for example, greater attention to theory, opening up of basic behavioral repertoires, broadening of analysis units with subsequently greater inclusion of behavioral categories, and increased range of environmental events to be considered). However, the most central aspect in which the concept of construct validity is applied is functional analysis of behavior. This, which essentially consists of the formulation and testing of explanatory hypotheses about the behavior in question (which resort to learning processes), constitutes in reality a process of construct validation in both its original and its present sense.

10

TREATMENT VALIDITY
The Issue of Utility

T hanks primarily to R. O. Nelson and S. C. Hayes, the concern for assessment quality has taken new directions in the behavioral approach. I refer here to what was originally called *treatment validity,* a concept proposed in the opening article of the first issue of the journal *Behavioral Assessment.*

According to Nelson and Hayes (1979b), if "the immediate practical value of behavioral assessment lies in its contribution to treatment," the main concern must be the question, "Does this assessment enhance treatment outcome?" They continue: "[An] adequate evaluation of behavioral assessment procedures frequently requires a demonstration that the treatment decisions produced by these procedures are maximally effective, given the treatment options available" (p. 12).

The idea appears also in another work by these authors: "Another way that behavioral assessment may be evaluated is in its contribution to treatment success, termed evaluation of treatment validity" (Nelson & Hayes, 1979a, p. 497). And two years later:

While the relationship between behavioral assessment and treatment has traditionally been acclaimed (Goldfried & Pomeranz, 1968), there is a need to demonstrate experimentally that specific methods of behavioral assessment actually lead to better treatment. Treatment validity can be determined for each step of behavioral assessment. . . . It can probably be said that any assessment device or conceptualization claiming to have applied value should be considered unproven until its treatment validity is experimentally demonstrated. Unfortunately, by this standard the applied value of virtually all of behavioral assessment is still "unproven." (Nelson & Hayes, 1981, pp. 25-26)

These authors, likewise, propose treatment validity as a problem of "utility" (p. 28).

These remarks, until now merely programmatic, had greater development and expansion a few years later. In 1986, Nelson and Hayes noted that the question regarding treatment validity was tied to behavior selection for treatment: "Does the selection of one target behavior lead to better treatment outcome than the selection of another target behavior? . . . Are better treatment results obtained if one target is selected rather than another target?" (1986b, pp. 28, 30).[1] In that text, they later moved to outline possible rocedures to arrive at an answer, which Hayes et al. (1986, 1987) deal with in detail.

Before touching upon some considerations with respect to these latest works, let us look at treatment validity from a more general perspective. We can agree that the contribution of assessment to treatment is absolutely central in evaluating behavioral assessment—and probably any diagnostic approach[2]—if *treatment* is understood in its broadest sense. Pretreatment assessment, according to most researchers, does no more than provide relevant information for the design of intervention. There is reason for concern that empirical research on the benefit is only beginning, and for urging "refinement of the relation between assessment and the selection of an appropriate therapeutic strategy" (Ciminero, 1977, p. 11).

But this concern goes far back and is found in the most traditional frameworks of assessment. Within applied psychology, industrial psychologists posed this kind of question several decades ago. In the clinical field, which most directly interests us right now, Hayes et al. fittingly cite Meehl (1959/1973a). Meehl wrote:

A final and most demanding way of putting the question, which is ultimately the practically significant one by which the contribution of our techniques must be judged, is the following: "If the test enables us to make reliable clear, differentiating statements which are accurate and which we cannot readily make from routinely available clinical bases of judgement . . . in what way, *and to what extent,* does this incremental advance information help us in treating the patient?" (p. 107).

Regarding this question, Meehl notes that "there is . . . no published empirical evidence."

The entire article by Meehl is strewn with interesting reflections on this subject. The following year, he returned to the theme: "Quite apart from the validity of current techniques . . . their pragmatic value is open to question. It is commonly believed that an accurate pretreatment personality assessment of his patient is of great value to the psychotherapist. It is not known to what extent, if at all, this is true" (Meehl, 1960/1971, p. 478). Meehl, using surveys done with the help of psychotherapists, continues to contribute information on the matter that is not in the least flattering.

Lang (1978a, 1978b) returns to this idea: It is not proven that therapeutic tasks are achieved better with diagnosis than without. This concerns an empirical problem to be investigated. Korchin and Schuldberg (1981) note that empirical evidence to date is small. Shapiro (1985) writes that "the contribution of psychological tests to the nature and usefulness of clinical decisions has, surprisingly, not been investigated" (p. 2). And McReynolds (1985) dedicates a good part of a recent work to this subject. Information he collected indicates a rather limited relation between assessment and therapy:

> Are tests helpful to the therapist? Amazingly, there has been little research on this crucial question. . . . One way in which it is often held that tests can be useful to a therapist—perhaps the most conventional way—is through pretherapy testing. The advance information provided by tests can help the therapist, so it is reasoned, to get under way faster and more effectively. This assumption has not been directly tested. . . . The best way to determine if assessment is helpful in psychotherapy would be to attack the problem empirically, through studies specifically designed to answer the question. Unfortunately, such studies, so far as I am aware, do not exist. . . . Not only has there been little research on the therapeutic utility of assessment, but amazingly little has been written on the subject. One looks in vain for books presenting the accumulated wisdom on the topic. (pp. 10, 11, 13)

In only a few articles or test manuals can one find specific attempts to relate diagnostic inferences to therapeutic decisions. McReynolds sees this lack as deriving from the traditional separation of assessment from treatment. Without a doubt, he points out, a diagnosis has value aside from its contribution to treatment success. However, this is a crucial point where some positive evidence turns up in neighboring fields (such as psychiatry). McReynolds concludes by reiterating that it will be necessary to reevaluate assessment instruments, specifically tracing their contribution to therapy success.

Logically, McReynolds's article refers to treatment validity as understood by Nelson and Hayes. Clarifying something that would soon become apparent, McReynolds (1985) points out that "treatment validity is not a fundamentally different type of validity, . . . rather, it refers to a given application of the notion of validity," and he sees a broader extension: "Though the concept of treatment validity was put forth with specific reference to behavioral assessment it appears to be applicable to all forms of pre-therapy assessment" (p. 18). We have seen this concern expressed in connection with nonbehavioral assessment, and many behaviorally oriented authors have spoken out. Besides the cited work by Ciminero, that by Mash (1979) can be quoted. For Mash, among the questions from which the value of behavioral assessment must be estimated, there is the following: "Does the quantity and quality of assessment contribute to the effectiveness of treatment?" (p. 27). Hartmann et al. (1979) speak of the usefulness of assessment in this same sense and cite articles from the behavioral approach that refer to the lack of evidence on the matter. "To summarize," writes Prout (1986), "it appears that the actual utility of assessment (behavioral or traditional) in planning and conducting treatment programs is unclear and has not been empirically demonstrated at this time" (p. 611). Because of this, the explicit reference to treatment validity in behavioral assessment is frequent and takes on different nuances. If, for example, Fernández-Ballesteros and Carrobles (1981b) put the emphasis, as many authors do, on treatment validity as the usefulness of assessment practice, then Haynes (1983), on the other hand, is interested in emphasizing its conceptual derivation, and he frames it within construct validity.

More recently, the creators of the concept of treatment validity have made a more detailed consideration of it in which several aspects are present. Hayes, Nelson, and Jarrett's works from 1986 and 1987 constitute an important step forward. The field of action is broadened. Treatment validity is applied to each and every aspect or stage of assessment: the classification schema, the methods, strategies and techniques, decision-making rules, and so on. On a more detailed level, there should be checks on repeated measurements, assessment in natural settings, the configuration of data graphs and its feedback to the client, the assumed advantages of frequency data, and so on. Nothing must escape the challenge to contribute to treatment results. Second, a series of designs to estimate treatment validity are proposed—the majority being group designs. Not only designs are proposed but also a systematization of them. Third, there are two conceptual advances. The mutual exchange between theory and treatment validity is emphasized: The theoretical models and the identified processes without a doubt guide the choice and configuration of the treatment programs; in turn, studies of treatment validity help to shed light on those models and processes and, therefore, contribute to scientific knowledge. Further, the expression *treatment validity* is replaced by *treatment utility,* a term used in the work of 1986 and that was the title of the article of the following year. Now *treatment utility* refers "to the degree to which assessment is shown to contribute to beneficial treatment outcome" (Hayes et al., 1987, p. 963).[3] According to what we have seen, this term progressively moved into the works of other authors concerned about this subject.

The discussion has moved from questioning the usefulness, alone, of assessment—that is, from comparing assessment to no assessment—to questioning *the relative usefulness of each type of assessment.* It is no longer enough to show that an assessment helps treatment. The question has become, Is it *more useful* than another type of assessment? One recalls Sechrest's (1963) concept of "incremental validity": Assessment procedures not only should have validity in improving a decision but should have *more* validity than the procedures already being used and, more generally, than any alternative procedure.

Many authors defend the greater usefulness of an individualized functional analysis as opposed to the standard nosological methods (e.g., Fernández-Ballesteros & Carrobles, 1987; Hersen, 1976; Mischel, 1968; Peterson, 1968; Schulte, 1973; Wolpe, 1977, 1986), but other authors doubt this alleged superiority and demand an empirical confrontation. The question posed by Emmelkamp (1981) hangs like the sword of Damocles over behavioral assessment: "Is treatment based on a functional analysis more effective than a standardized treatment program?" (p. 252; see also Hartmann et al., 1979; Haynes, 1983, 1986, 1990, 1991; Kanfer & Nay, 1982; Nathan, 1981). In fact, there exist on this topic discouraging data (e.g., Schulte & Wittchen, 1988). Nelson and Hayes (1986b) and Hayes et al. (1986) address this *fundamental* question. Nelson (1987) went back to it a year later and then wrote a monograph (Nelson, 1988) on the subject that earned a special section in the *Journal of Psychopathology and Behavioral Assessment,* where Turkat (1988) and, above all, Haynes (1988) added interesting contributions. But to go into a comparison of the efficiency for therapy of diverse diagnostic approaches here takes us away from our line of argument. We must leave this theme for future research.

Some Controversial Issues

Notwithstanding the above, Hayes et al.'s 1987 publication—which, at the same time, seems to be a type of coronation of what has been done up to now on treatment utility—reveals two important deviations. One has to do with the relation between treatment utility and psychometric standards; the other, with the concept of utility itself.

First, repeating what Cronbach and Gleser (1965) pointed out (see also Michel & Mai, 1968), Hayes et al. realize that an essentially applied approach that includes treatment utility moves a bit away from quality standards that, like reliability and validity, are more concerned with soundness or appropriateness of the diagnosis than with its usefulness for the therapeutic process. They also go back to something from Cronbach and Gleser that Wiggins, among others, emphasized: *One cannot wait for a "perfect" assessment in order to demonstrate its utility with regard to a certain problem.* Contradicting themselves when claiming to give theoretical importance to treatment validity, Hayes et al. take things further. The same thing mentioned above with respect to the concept of accuracy happens here: In some moments they seem to separate treatment utility completely from the dimensions of reliability and validity, up to the point at which procedures that are neither reliable nor valid might be useful:

> The relation between psychometric criteria and treatment utility is often open to question. Thus, there seems to be little reason to insist in principle that treatment utility must be the last step in the evaluation of a given assessment device, distinction, or approach. Treatment utility is shown by a well-designed study, regardless of the state of previous psychometric evaluations. (Hayes et al., 1987, p. 972)

However, Hayes et al. have to add that "this is not to say that reliability and validity should be ignored in treatment utility research," because if utility is not proven in a given study, this could be because the assessment instruments used do not have sufficient psychometric support. When these authors anticipate finding utility without reliability or validity, what they really do is warn against the sole emphasis on the instruments or the diagnostic report instead of emphasis on *the assessment process.* This is certainly a deficiency to which we shall return, but it does not allow us to separate utility from quality standards. Barrios (1988) rightly sees this as a dead-end street:

> In the treatment validity model, we are evaluating the quality of our assessment data on the basis of experimental data [the "well-designed" studies that Hayes et al. mention above]. The obvious question is: How do we evaluate the quality of the experimental data on which we base our evaluation of our assessment data? According to the model, we do so by inspecting the integrity or validity of the design of the experiment (e.g., Campbell & Stanley, 1966; Cook & Campbell, 1979). A thorough inspection of the integrity of the experiment's design does, however, call for an inspection of the integrity of the experiment's measures. The treatment validity model offers no guidelines for carrying out such an inspection. It appears, then, that the treatment validity model begs the question of how to evaluate the quality of assessment data. (p. 34)

Hayes et al. (1987) realize this danger, writing, "It is impossible to build a science of assessment totally on treatment utility alone. Knowing the effect on treatment outcome itself requires assessment, and that means that treatment utility must ultimately be based on measures that are themselves not validated in this manner" (p. 972). This ought to lead to the conclusion that, to escape making estimation of assessment utility (contribution to treatment effects) impossible, we must preserve reliability and validity as quality standards both independent and related to utility. This is exactly what the psychometric theory of utility has done (Cronbach & Gleser, 1965; Wiggins, 1973): Validity is *necessary* but not **sufficient** for utility (nor is the relation linear between them, insofar as utility recognizes additional parameters). But, with respect to these remarks, the second point of conflict emerges.

Wanting to emphasize the originality of their stance, Hayes et al. (1987) attempt to separate themselves from the psychometric concept of utility:

> The treatment utility of assessment deserves to be termed a type of utility because it relates closely to the functional thrust of that psychometric term. . . . [Nevertheless] the need to qualify the word utility with the adjective treatment is justified by two facts. First, utility has been almost exclusively evaluated in terms of personnel decisions (e.g., Wiggins, 1973). The issues and methods involved in demonstrating the impact of assessment on treatment outcomes differ significantly from the methods appropriate to the analysis of personnel decisions. Second, in personnel matters the concept of utility has come to refer primarily to the cost-benefit ratio of assessment strategies. . . . The treatment utility of assessment is not primarily a matter of cost-benefit analysis but of the demonstration of a particular type of benefit. (p. 964)

In order to be able to weigh these remarks, we must necessarily refer to aspects of the psychometric concept of utility, as discussed below.

The determination of utility, defined as "the relative value of an outcome with respect to the set of other possible outcomes" (AERA, APA, & NCME, 1985, p. 94), is now a central matter within the psychometric approach. Utility has never been limited to the scope of personnel decisions. One pioneer work on this topic, by Meehl and Rosen (1955), appears in a clinical context. These authors explicitly emphasize that the selection process in clinical psychology must be distinguished from the selection process in the industrial field, exactly with regard to assigning meanings and values to each type of possible outcome. A misunderstanding could result from the seminal work *Psychological Tests and Personnel Decisions* by Cronbach and Gleser (1957, 1965). Just as these authors point out that they use the term *test* to refer to any procedure for information gathering— including, for example, interviews, biographical inquiries, and physical measures—Cronbach and Gleser (1965) point out that "the reference to 'personnel decisions' in our title may suggest that we are concerned only with the decisions of industrial and military personnel management, but this is not the case. Our discussion embraces problems of guidance, clinical assessment, and teaching. We are concerned with the use of tests used in all these types of decision" (p. 7). There is explicit reference to therapeutic decisions. On the other hand, it must be recalled that the principal scope of application for Cronbach is the educational, and for Gleser, the clinical. Soon there appeared in clinical psychology the echo of the pioneer statements on decision theory and on the determination of utility in choice of therapy (Arthur, 1966). This problem currently recovers before a more or less imminent future of budget cutbacks, demonstration of results, and assumption of competencies that clinical assessment should face (e.g., Ziskin, 1986).

The problem of utility is the same in treatment utility as in personnel selection. It is necessary to return to this point. Utility concerns concrete diagnostic information aiming to optimize outcomes obtained when some people are put into set treatments. Remember that Cronbach and Gleser give the term *treatment* its broadest meaning; the stimulus complex that constitutes a determined work position *is a treatment* to which a person is submitted. In the therapeutic field, some indicators of success are naturally interesting—for example, the disappearance of symptoms, improved family relationships, feelings of well-being. In the case of job selection, other indicators are important—performance, stability in the position, job satisfaction, and so on—but nothing here varies the basic schema.

The psychometric approach to utility has tended to give excessive importance to economic criteria (e.g., Cronbach & Gleser, 1965), but it is also certain that writers have repeatedly insisted that this must be one single criterion. Such excessive importance can be easily understood. First, it must be recalled that decisions about work are commonly made from an institutional perspective and not an individual one. Second, the relative facility in using economic criteria make them a constant reductionist temptation. Third, and related to this, it is difficult to fix values of utility—the Achilles' heel of decision theory—in many criterion areas. But this recurrent difficulty must not intimidate us (Wiggins, 1973). Something similar to what happened in the discussion about criterion variables in the framework of predictive validity happens here: What comes first is their relevance; second is their ease of access.

More than one misunderstanding appears when Hayes et al. (1987), attempting to differentiate its meaning from the psychometric concept of utility, write that "the treatment utility of assessment is not primarily a matter of cost-benefit analysis but of the demonstration of a particular type of benefit" (p. 964). If they were concerned only with *demonstrating outcomes,* their concept of treatment utility would not be essentially different from that of internal validity (in determining causal relationships) or from that of external validity (in determining generalization effects). Then they could well return to the expression *treatment validity.* Yet utility analysis concerns *benefits*; an evaluation is required for each possible outcome. To assess benefit is to go beyond proving to weighing, that is, to ascribing utility values. What else would make us prefer some targets over others and make us give more importance to some therapeutic achievements than to others? Speaking of benefits involves speaking of costs—again, not only economic costs but also personal, subjective costs, and social costs. The concept of net benefit includes that of cost. To think otherwise would be rather naive. The determination of treatment utility concerns evaluating therapeutic outcomes with respect to "assessment" and other costs. It *does* concern a cost-benefit analysis.

It was precisely in this way that the problem of utility was posed in behavioral assessment, beyond the perspective of treatment utility and just as Wiggins (1973) claimed. Haynes (1979) points out that frequently high costs, of a varied nature, which an individualized behavioral pretreatment assessment many times brings with it, may not be compensated by therapeutic benefits. Still, empirical evidence is lacking. "Ultimately," add Haynes and Wilson (1979), "a cost-benefit analysis (cost of assessing individual differences and benefits in improved effectiveness) will dictate the utility of emphasizing individual differences" (p. 7). This same idea appears in the work by Haynes in 1983, which focused on an evaluation of instrumentation (for example, high costs of behavioral observation and recording). A more recent work makes a more complete and detailed critical review of instrumentation, with recommendations for increasing its utility (Haynes, 1986). For their part, Kanfer and Nay (1982), who clearly approach the problem of utility along the lines set out by Meehl and Rosen (1955) and Cronbach and Gleser (1957, 1965), summarized by Wiggins (1973), analyze costs into different types and categories: personal costs for the client, social costs, and administrative costs.

Recently, Barrios (1988) has also returned to this line of thought. He emphasizes that "the ultimate worth of an assessment does not . . . lie in its precision; the ultimate worth of an assessment lies in its usefulness. . . . The measurement concept of utility subsumes and supersedes the measurement concept of precision. It is, therefore, the measurement concept of utility which has the final say as to the value of an assessment (e.g., Barrios & Hartmann, 1986; Nelson & Hayes, 1986[b])" (p. 7; see also Nelson & Hayes, 1981). One cannot help but compare this quotation to Cronbach and Gleser's (1965) emphasis that "the value of a test can be stated only in terms of the specific type of decision problem, the strategy employed, the evaluation attached to the outcome, and the cost of testing"

(p. 32), and that "the contribution of the test over and above available bases for the same judgement should be the criterion of its worth, rather than some measure of its accuracy, standing alone" (p. 36). Barrios (1988) in turn emphasizes the importance of costs tied to treatment, beyond the actual costs of assessment. These two must be targets for evaluation. He also points out the limited proof of utility of behavioral assessment throughout its several stages. After a brief review, he concludes that "there is little doubt . . . that the methodology available for assessing utility (e.g., Wiggins, 1973) continues to be relevant to the field of behavioral assessment" (Barrios & Hartmann, 1986, p. 93), and he finishes with a very interesting observation: Until now, in any of the approaches to data evaluation in behavioral assessment, there has been no explicit formulation of the concept of utility and no consequential elaboration of it that would lead to the exploitation of all its possibilities (Barrios, 1988).

I cannot but agree, and conclude together with Barrios and other authors cited earlier, that the psychometric approach constitutes, in the theme of decision theory and its concept of utility, a great aid for behavioral assessment.

Conclusions

This chapter has introduced utility in behavioral assessment through the concept of *treatment validity* or, more recently, *treatment utility,* as defined by Nelson, Hayes, and others. The issue of treatment utility—that is, of the degree to which assessment contributes to improving treatment outcomes—is not a new one in clinical psychology, and its proposal and expansion in behavioral assessment undoubtedly must be considered as beneficial. Among the developments that the concept includes is, for example, the question about the relative efficiency of a behavioral assessment approach with respect to other assessment approaches or models.

Without denying the merit of the notion of treatment utility, I have nevertheless called attention to recent statements that seem incorrect and potentially harmful for future developments. One is the attempt to separate treatment utility from metric standards of quality. To the contrary, these standards are needed if we want to avoid entering into a dead-end track: attempting to judge the quality of assessment according to treatment utility, when treatment utility must in turn be judged with the help of assessment instruments that involve quality guarantees.

Another dangerous development is the attempt to separate treatment utility from the psychometric concept of utility. Treatment utility constitutes a particular case in the broadest framework of the notion of utility applied to psychological assessment by authors such as Cronbach, Gleser, and Meehl. This point of view appears to agree with the perspective with which behavioral assessors other than Nelson et al. consider utility.

Notes

1. In reality, Nelson and Hayes later waver over whether or not to consider this question as pertinent to treatment validity (e.g., Hayes et al., 1986). At any rate, this cannot be answered before the level of analysis at which one is working is clarified (for example, symptomatic or syndromatic).

2. While commenting on Nelson and Hayes's first developments on treatment validity, Cone (1982) points out that "it is reasonable to expect treatment validity concepts to be applied to other forms of assessment as well" (p. 77).

3. Cone (1989) has recently suggested replacing the term *treatment utility* with *intervention utility*, because the scope of the word *intervention* is usually broader (for example, in educational and organizational settings). This suggestion is certainly interesting.

11

SUMMARY

Throughout the consideration of the possible applications of psychometric standards in behavioral assessment presented in this volume, I have responded to and refuted criticisms of such applications. "As devastating as . . . criticisms of the psychometric model may appear to be", writes Barrios (1988), "they are, upon careful consideration, not very devastating at all. Each of the criticisms stem from a misunderstanding of the nature and application of the model, which upon clarification lessens or eliminates the criticism" (p. 32). This book's systematic run through the psychometric standards of quality applied to assessment brings me to a similar conclusion, though I judge that not all the criticisms have arisen from misunderstanding. Questionable assumptions and biased practices surely existed in classical psychometric assessment; behavioral assessors helped by denouncing these. Still, behavioral assessment has been insufficiently conscious of the development in psychometric thought during the last decades; those deficiencies have been faced—and almost completely overcome. Modern positions clearly come closer to the behavioral orientations, and the opportunity to applaud behavioral contributions is not missed. If

I were to make a single criticism of some writers on behavioral assessment—not all—it would be that they are not paying enough attention to the most recent theoretical and methodological developments of psychometric assessment. If we take a careful look at them, the panorama looks undoubtedly more interesting and hopeful.

In the review of the principal psychometric standards of quality and some related matters, the discussion had a directional line. The issue of reliability, whatever be the universe within which one wants to generalize, is understood in the framework of a more fundamental question: Am I measuring what I want to measure and not something else? That is, it is understood within the framework of validity. And validity, understood as the legitimation of the inferences that may be taken from the results given by assessment devices, is a unitary concept, identified with construct validity. Behind the deceiving appearance of a "new type" of validity, the reflections and formulations of Cronbach and Meehl (1955), already partially contained in the first (1954) *Standards,* really signify a profound restatement of the concept of validity. Loevinger (1957) realized very early the meaning of this little "Copernican revolution," which has done nothing but mature over the years.

Yet construct validity was born not solely to rescue the rationality of the diagnostic praxis (e.g., Cattell, 1964), but also to empower its utility. With regard to this latter pretension arises the repeatedly confirmed poor contribution of many constructs in tasks of prediction and "incremental validity," which Mischel (1968) knew how to collect and use very well. Nevertheless, the issue does not end here. There are many reasons for the failure of those constructs used in certain ways, in certain designs, and for certain objectives. Construct validity forms part of the attempt at a scientific explanation of the behavior being studied, with the goal of allowing a more rational, better founded, more effective action.

The concept of construct validity—or of validity alone—continues to progress. Why? Because, according to what we have seen, it has also had an evolution, although clearly stated from the start, that has considerably changed its countenance.

The original emphasis was on empirically supporting the explanatory concepts that supposedly underlay the responses to an assessment instrument. The instrument-construct pair was the fundamental issue. With this in mind, the traditional tendency of ensuring the scientific quality of assessment via the validity of instruments was continued. Nevertheless, little by little, researchers began to realize the inadequacy of this point of view. This occurred to the extent that they began to notice the necessary *contextualization* of validity (e.g., Cole & Moss, 1989; Cronbach, 1988). This means that validity data, as well as any explanatory theoretical model, cannot be automatically applied to a new problem. The recourse is not algorithmic, but rather heuristic (Westmeyer, 1984; see also Cronbach, 1988; Tenopyr & Oeltjen, 1982; in addition, see Messick, 1989, on "validity generalization" arguments). In 1966, Merz pointed out that a validity coefficient is not something that can be mechanically applied, *that it is only an indication, a hypothesis for facing a new, hitherto unknown situation.* Merz also brought up the consequences: The applied psychologist must be a scientist who researches the field in which he or she works. Cronbach returns time and again to this idea, which plays a central role in his 1975 article. Recalling Dunnette (1967), he tells us that formal theories do not give us fixed rules of action, but rather are aids for thinking about what a response in a given situation can mean. "The published research merely provides the interpreter with some facts and concepts. He has to combine these with his other knowledge about the persons he tests and the assignments or adjustment problems that confront them, to decide what interpretations are warranted" (Cronbach, 1971, p. 445). In the greater majority of the cases, what is indicated is a "local validation" (p. 486).

In his 1975 article, Cronbach takes these reflections to an extreme, so to speak, by questioning even the attainability of scientific laws in a discipline such as psychology. In any case, the ideas stated above appear and are broadened: "When we give proper weight to local conditions, any generalization is a working hypothesis, not a conclusion" (Cronbach, 1975, p. 125; see also Morales, 1988; Pawlik, 1976). "When the universe changes, we have to go beyond our actuarial rule. As Meehl (1957) has said, when we step outside the range of our experience, we have to use our heads" (Cronbach, 1975, pp. 125-126). Then the explanatory concepts will not be direct solutions to the problems presented, but rather an aid for "using our heads." These reflections contain a fundamental contribution: the need to open ourselves as much as possible to a prehypothetical observation and exploration, to take ourselves back to the "context of discovery," prior to the "context of justification," where hypothetico-deductive thought functions (Reichenbach, 1938). These observations return later in other works (e.g., Cronbach, 1980, 1984a, 1989; Cronbach & Snow, 1977). Cronbach's 1975 contributions had a clear impact on other authors (e.g., Glass & Ellett, 1980; and Morales, 1988, who underlines the temporality and, therefore, the expiration of data and conclusions). Even the American Psychological Association has insisted on regarding with the appropriate distance the data belonging to test manuals in their application to particular problems (e.g., APA, AERA, & NCME, 1974). And an author of the status of Anastasi (1985) writes that the common theme that emerges from developments of psychological measurement over the last 50 years is precisely that of the need for contextualization.

These lines of reflection have had other expressions. For example, some authors emphasize the unavoidable *human element* in assessment and, therefore, the problem of *the assessor's validity* (e.g., Landorf, 1976, 1978; Pulver, 1978b; Sines, 1959/1971). This concern constitutes a central issue within the controversy between clinical and statistical approaches. Meehl's (1954) following remark is especially pertinent here:

> The introduction of some special "clinical utility" as a surrogate to validation is inadmissible. If the clinical utility is really established and not merely proclaimed, it will have been established by procedures which have all the earmarks of an acceptable validation study. If not, it is a weasel phrase and we ought not get by with it. (p. 138)

What is important now is that the controversy between clinical and statistical approaches brings us to a crossroad, well described by Holt (1984) in the following text:

> However successful a team of actuaries may be, they need not understand any of the behavior they successfully predict once given the desired data about the subjects. They do not have to know anything about how the behavior is organized and determined, what significance it has in the lives of the persons involved, or how it could be affected in any way; nor is their work likely to yield anything of the kind—only reasonably effective predictions. Clinicians, by contrast, are full of hypotheses about these psychologically more nutritious matters, but are typically unable to frame them in testing fashion or to adduce any evidence that these hypotheses are right or wrong. (p. 185)

Does construct validation help in light of all these questions? Without a doubt, to the extent that we do not interpret it as a search for correlations between constructs and instruments, but see it as a *process of exploring, constructing hypothetical explanatory models, and testing them*. It is in this sense that Cronbach and Meehl (1955) state that the research in construct validation matches the scientific procedure of theory development and testing. This is precisely the way in which Kelly (1955) viewed clinical diagnostics, a way that Peterson (1968), from a behavioral perspective, knew how to valuate. Exactly this, as Holt pointed out, is missing from the clinical approach, and the psychometric approach also needs it. If validity related to the instruments is—although undoubtedly desirable—insufficient for assuring the quality of a new concrete diagnostic undertaking (Cronbach, 1982; Fernández-Ballesteros, 1985; Fernández-Ballesteros & Maciá, 1983; Vizcarro, 1987), we must concentrate on the validation of the diagnosis itself, ensuring the quality of the *assessment process*. In this task construct validity—that is, we repeat, validity alone—acquires its clearest meaning. *Every psychological assessment must provide its own validation* (Silva, 1988). Arising first in a context of discovery, explanatory hypotheses are then placed in the context of justification, where they must be tested (above all, by trying to "falsify" or reject them).

What is proposed in the concept of functional analysis of behavior, the central point of behavioral assessment, is nothing else. The above leads me to state that we must pay more attention to the assessment process as decision making (which at the same time brings us to the doorstep of the problems of utility), as has been insisted upon lately with respect to behavioral assessment. For example, Evans and Wilson's (1983) article "Behavioral Assessment and Decision Making: A Theoretical Analysis" claims to restate the concept and praxis of behavioral assessment in those terms. Barrios (1988), among others, supports this reorientation and denounces what "heretofore . . . has been a conspiracy of silence among us with regard to our decision-making strategies. To sensitively and systematically study the worth of assessment data, we must delineate the models we are using to arrive at treatment decisions" (p. 35). Kanfer is also strongly propagating this idea (e.g., Kanfer & Busemeyer, 1982). The psychometric concept of validity, in its most recent evolution, helps us to redirect our attention toward the process of behavioral assessment, which, once again, is not essentially different from the general process of psychological assessment. At the same time, it also contributes a great number of suggestions with respect to concrete strategies and techniques.

Allow me to summarize, very concisely, the primary conclusions reached in this volume. Throughout, the following points have been made clear:

1. In behavioral assessment, just as in psychological assessment in general, both idiographic and nomothetic approaches are necessary.
2. Likewise, behavioral assessment requires both "criterion reference" and "norm reference."
3. Once free of the assumptions regarding behavioral consistency and stability linked to the classical conception of reliability, this concept is not only applicable to behavioral assessment but necessary for its development.
4. Behavioral assessment cannot get away from criterion-oriented validity, especially with regard to prediction of treatment outcomes.
5. Behavioral assessment cannot disregard constructs. Far from avoiding psychological constructs by falling back on content validity, this concept, as we have seen, necessarily brings us to constructs; the problems of content validity are in reality problems of construct validity.
6. Construct validation is present in the nucleus of behavioral assessment, because it expresses what is understood as functional analysis of behavior: a

process of construction, postulation, and testing of explanatory hypotheses about specific behaviors.

7. To the extent that the concept of construct validity is likewise identified with the psychometric concept of validity and, more appropriately, with the validation of the process of assessment, it unifies the experimental and correlational perspectives of psychological assessment. All assessment essentially consists of hypothesis development and testing about a person's behavior. The experimental and correlational perspectives constitute different and complementary approaches within such a task (Cronbach, 1957).

8. Throughout *treatment validity* (or *treatment utility*), the psychometric concept of utility is also present in behavioral assessment, marking important courses for future research.

Is it appropriate to continue to postulate methodological differences between behavioral and psychometric assessment that are more apparent than real? More generally, is it appropriate to attempt to separate one branch of assessment from another? My response is emphatically negative, and with that I fall in line with many behavioral assessors, as well as, more generally, with a clear tendency toward integration. Cone (1981b) poses an unmuffled threat of "secession": "While unlikely, it would not be surprising to see a . . . separatist movement erupt in behavioral assessment, with radical behavioral assessors forming their own clearly identifiable discipline or subdiscipline within the overall framework of the study of behavior from a natural science perspective" (p. 64; see also Barrett et al., 1986). I completely disagree with this, and this book signifies an attempt to prevent it. In my opinion, the separatist movement would be notably impoverished and would have negative repercussions on behavioral assessment and on psychological assessment as a whole. Instead, I completely share Mischel's (1988) invitation to behavioral assessment, that it be "responsive to a larger science" that impedes it from falling into a "narrow provincialism" (p. 128), as well as the final reflections by McReynolds in his 1986 work, where, together with emphasizing the undeniable contributions of the behavioral approach to the discipline of assessment, he points out:

Behavioral assessment is, however, a part of the whole. When viewed in terms of its historical antecedents and its current functions and problems, it has much in common with other approaches to assessment. It is best conceptualized in terms of its place in the larger picture. (p. 72)

REFERENCES

Allport, G. W. (1937). *Personality: A psychological interpretation.* New York: Holt.

Allport, G. W. (1942). *The use of personal documents in psychological science.* New York: Social Science Research Council.

Allport, G. W. (1962). The general and the unique in psychological science. *Journal of Personality, 30,* 405-422.

Alvira, F., Avia, M. D., Calvo, R., & Morales, J. F. (1979). *Los dosa métodos de las ciencias sociales.* Madrid: Centro de Investigaciones Sociológicas.

American Educational Research Association (AERA), American Psychological Association (APA), & National Council on Measurement in Education (NCME). (1985). *Standards for educational and psychological testing.* Washington, DC: American Psychological Association.

American Psychiatric Association. (1980). *Diagnostic and statistical manual of mental disorders* (3rd ed.). Washington, DC: Author.

American Psychiatric Association. (1987). *Diagnostic and statistical manual of mental disorders* (3rd ed., rev.). Washington, DC: Author.

American Psychological Association (APA). (1954). *Technical recommendations for psychological tests and diagnostic techniques.* Washington, DC: Author.

American Psychological Association (APA). (1966). Standards for educational and psychological tests and manuals. In D. N. Jackson & S. Messick (Eds.), *Problems in human assessment.* Washington, DC: Author.

American Psychological Association (APA), American Educational Research Association (AERA), & National Council on Measurement in Education (NCME). (1974). *Standards for educational and psychological tests.* Washington, DC: American Psychological Association.

Anastasi, A. (1967). Psychology, psychologists, and psychological testing. *American Psychologist, 22,* 297-306.

Anastasi, A. (1976). *Psychological testing* (4th ed.). New York: Macmillan.

Anastasi, A. (1985). Mental measurement: Some emerging trends. In J. V. Mitchell (Ed.), *The ninth mental measurements yearbook* (Vol. 1). Lincoln: University of Nebraska Press.

Anastasi, A. (1986). Evolving concepts of test validation. *Annual Review of Psychology, 37,* 1-15.

Anastasi, A. (1988). *Psychological testing* (6th ed.). New York: Macmillan.

Anastasi, A., et al. (1984). Commentaries on the development of technical standards for educational and psychological testing. In C. D. Daves (Ed.), *The uses and misuses of tests.* San Francisco: Jossey-Bass.

Angoff, W. H. (1974). Criterion-referencing, norm referencing, and the SAT. *College Board Review, 92,* 3-5,21.

Angoff, W. H. (1988). Validity: An evolving concept. In H. Wainer & H. I. Braun (Eds.), *Test validity.* Hillsdale, NJ: Lawrence Erlbaum.

Arthur, A. Z. (1966). A decision-making approach to psychological assessment in the clinic. *Journal of Consulting Psychology, 30,* 435-438.

Arthur, A. Z. (1969). Diagnostic testing and the new alternatives. *Psychological Bulletin, 72,* 183-192.

Baer, D. M., Wolf, M. M., & Risley, T. R. (1968). Some current dimensions of applied behavior analysis. *Journal of Applied Behavior Analysis, 1,* 91-97.

Baer, D. M., Wolf, M. M., & Risley, T. R. (1987). Some still-current dimensions of applied behavior analysis. *Journal of Applied Behavior Analysis, 20,* 313-327.

Barlow, D. H., & Hersen, M. (1984). *Single case experimental designs: Strategies for studying behavior change* (2nd ed.). New York: Pergamon.

Barrett, B. H., Johnston, J. M., & Pennypacker, H. S. (1986). Behavior: Its units, dimensions, and measurement. In R. O. Nelson & S. C. Hayes (Eds.), *Conceptual foundations of behavioral assessment.* New York: Guilford.

Barrios, B. A. (1988). On the changing nature of behavioral assessment. In A. S. Bellack & M. Hersen (Eds.), *Behavioral assessment: A practical handbook* (3rd ed.). New York: Pergamon.

Barrios, B. A., & Hartmann, D. P. (1986). The contributions of traditional assessment: Concepts, issues, and methodologies. In R. O. Nelson & S. C. Hayes (Eds.), *Conceptual foundations of behavioral assessment.* New York: Guilford.

Barrios, B. A., & Shigetomi, C. C. (1985). Assessment of children's fears: A critical review. In T. R. Kratochwill (Ed.), *Advances in school psychology* (vol. 4). Hillsdale, NJ: Lawrence Erlbaum.

Baum, C. G., Forehand, R., & Zegoib, L. E. (1979). A review of observer reactivity in adult-child interactions. *Journal of Behavioral Assessment, 1,* 167-177.

Baumann, U. (1981). Differentielle Therapiestudien und Indikation. In U. Baumann (Ed.), *Indikation zur Psychotherapie: Perspektiven für Praxis und Forschung.* Munich: Urban & Schwarzenberg.

Bayés, R. (1978). *Una introducción al método científico en psicología.* Barcelona: Fontanella.

Bechtoldt, H. P. (1967). Construct validity: A critique. In D. N. Jackson & S. Messick (Eds.), *Problems in human assessment.* New York: McGraw-Hill. (Original work published 1959)

Beck, L. W. (1950). Constructions and inferred entities. *Philosophy of Science, 17,* 74-86.

Bellack, A. S., & Hersen, M. (1988). Future directions of behavioral assessment. In A. S. Bellack & M. Hersen (Eds.), *Behavioral assessment: A practical handbook* (3rd ed.). New York: Pergamon.

Bellack, A. S., Hersen, M., & Lamparski, D. (1979). Role-play tests for assessing social skills: Are they valid? Are they useful? *Journal of Consulting and Clinical Psychology, 47*, 670-678.

Bem, D. J. (1983). Constructing a theory of the triple topology: Some (second) thoughts on nomothetic and idiographic approaches to personality. *Journal of Personality, 51*, 566-577.

Berlyne, D. E. (1965). *Structure and direction in thinking.* New York: John Wiley.

Bernstein, D. A., & Nietzel, M. T. (1982). *Introducción a la psicología clínica.* Mexico City: McGraw-Hill.

Bijou, S. W., & Peterson, R. F. (1971). Functional analysis in the assessment of children. In P. McReynolds (Ed.), *Advances in psychological assessment* (Vol. 2). Palo Alto, CA: Science & Behavior.

Binning, J. F., & Barrett, G. V. (1989). Validity of personnel decisions: A conceptual analysis of the inferential and evidential bases. *Journal of Applied Psychology, 74*, 478-494.

Brinberg, D., & McGrath, J. E. (1985). *Validity and the research process.* Beverly Hills, CA: Sage.

Burns, G. L. (1980). Indirect measurement and behavioral assessment: A case for social behaviorism psychometrics. *Behavioral Assessment, 2*, 197-206.

Byrne, D. (1964). Assessing personality variables and their alteration. In P. Worchel & D. Byrne (Eds.), *Personality change.* New York: John Wiley.

Campbell, D. T. (1960). Recommendations for APA test standards regarding construct, trait, or discriminant validity. *American Psychologist, 15*, 546-553.

Campbell, D. T., & Fiske, D. W. (1959). Convergent and discriminant validation by the multitrait-multimethod matrix. *Psychological Bulletin, 56*, 81-105.

Campbell, D. T., & Stanley, J. C. (1963). Experimental and quasi-experimental designs for research on teaching. In N. L. Gage (Ed.), *Handbook of research on teaching.* Chicago: Rand McNally.

Campbell, D. T., & Stanley, J. C. (1966). *Experimental and quasi-experimental designs for research.* Chicago: Rand McNally.

Carbonell, E. J. (1987). *La evaluación psicológica: líneas actuales de investigación a partir del estudio de su literatura científica. Una aproximación cienciométrica.* Unpublished doctoral thesis, University of Valencia.

Carlson, R. (1971). Where is the person in personality research? *Psychological Bulletin, 75*, 203-219.

Carmines, E. G., & Zeller, R. A. (1979). *Reliability and validity assessment.* London: Sage.

Carver, R. P. (1974). Two dimensions of tests: Psychometric and edumetric. *American Psychologist, 29*, 512-518.

Cattell, R. B. (1964). Validity and reliability: A proposed more basic set of concepts. *Journal of Educational Psychology, 55*, 1-22.

Cattell, R. B. (1970). *The scientific analysis of personality.* Harmondsworth, UK: Penguin.

Cattell, R. B. (1986). The psychometric properties of tests: Consistency, validity, and efficiency. In R. B. Cattell & R. C. Johnson (Eds.), *Functional psychological testing: Principles and instruments.* New York: Brunner/Mazel.

Cattell, R. B., & Tsujioka, B. (1964). The importance of factor-trueness and validity, versus homogeneity and orthogonality, in test scales. *Educational and Psychological Measurement, 24*, 3-30.

Caws, P. (1965). *The philosophy of science: A systematic account.* Princeton, NJ: Van Nostrand.

Chamberlain, T. C. (1965). The method of multiple working hypotheses. *Science, 148,* 754-759.

Chassan, J. B. (1960). Statistical inference and the single case in clinical design. *Psychiatry, 23,* 173-184.

Chassan, J. B. (1979). *Research design in clinical psychology and psychiatry.* New York: Irvington.

Chow, S. L. (1987). Science, ecological validity and experimentation. *Journal for the Theory of Social Behavior, 17,* 181-194.

Ciminero, A. R. (1977). Behavioral assessment: An overview. In A. R. Ciminero, K. S. Calhoun, & H. E. Adams (Eds.), *Handbook of behavioral assessment.* New York: John Wiley.

Ciminero, A. R. (1986). Behavioral assessment: An overview. In A. R. Ciminero, K. S. Calhoun, & H. E. Adams (Eds.), *Handbook of behavioral assessment* (2nd ed.). New York: John Wiley.

Ciminero, A. R., Calhoun, K. S., & Adams, H. E. (Eds.). (1986). *Handbook of behavioral assessment* (2nd ed.). New York: John Wiley.

Coates, T. J., & Thoresen, C. E. (1978). Using generalizability theory in behavioral observation. *Behavior Therapy, 9,* 605-613.

Cole, N. S., & Moss, P. A. (1989). Bias in test use. In R. L. Linn (Ed.), *Educational measurement* (3rd ed.). New York: American Council on Education, Macmillan, & Collier Macmillan.

Cone, J. D. (1976). Multitrait-multimethod matrices in behavioral assessment. In *Behavioral assessment: The relevance of traditional psychometric procedures.* Symposium conducted at the meeting of the American Psychological Association, Washington, DC.

Cone, J. D. (1977a). Confounded comparisons in triple response mode assessment research. In *Issues in anxiety and behavior assessment: Triple response mode approaches.* Symposium conducted at the meeting of the Association for the Advancement of Behavior Therapy, Atlanta, GA.

Cone, J. D. (1977b). The relevance of reliability and validity for behavioral assessment. *Behavior Therapy, 8,* 411-426.

Cone, J. D. (1978a). The Behavioral Assessment Grid (BAG): A conceptual framework and a taxonomy. *Behavior Therapy, 9,* 882-888.

Cone, J. D. (1978b). Truth and sensitivity in behavioral assessment. In *Strategies in evaluating the quality of behavioral assessment.* Symposium conducted at the meeting of the Association for the Advancement of Behavior Therapy, Chicago.

Cone, J. D. (1979). Confounded comparisons in triple response mode assessment research. *Behavioral Assessment, 1,* 85-95.

Cone, J. D. (1981a). Algunas observaciones sobre las comparaciones entre métodos en evaluación conductual. In R. Fernández-Ballesteros & J. A. I. Carrobles (Eds.), *Evaluación conductual. Metodología y aplicaciones.* Madrid: Pirámide.

Cone, J. D. (1981b). Psychometric considerations. In M. Hersen & A. S. Bellack (Eds.), *Behavioral assessment: A practical handbook* (2nd ed.). New York: Pergamon.

Cone, J. D. (1982). Validity of direct observation assessment procedures. In D. P. Hartmann (Ed.), *Using observers to study behavior.* San Francisco: Jossey-Bass.

Cone, J. D. (1986). Idiographic, nomothetic, and related perspectives in behavioral assessment. In R. O. Nelson & S. C. Hayes (Eds.), *Conceptual foundations of behavioral assessment.* New York: Guilford.

Cone, J. D. (1987a). Behavioral assessment: Some things old, some things new, some things borrowed? *Behavioral Assessment, 9,* 1-4.

Cone, J. D. (1987b). Consideraciones "psicométricas" en la evaluación conductual. In R. Fernández-Ballesteros & J. A. I. Carrobles (Eds.), *Evaluación conductual. Metodología y aplicaciones* (3rd ed.). Madrid: Pirámide.

Cone, J. D. (1988). Psychometric considerations and the multiple models of behavioral assessment. In A. S. Bellack & M. Hersen (Eds.), *Behavioral assessment: A practical handbook* (3rd ed.). New York: Pergamon.

Cone, J. D. (1989). Is there utility for treatment utility? *American Psychologist, 44,* 1241-1242.

Cone, J. D., & Hawkins, R. P. (1977a). Current status and future directions in behavioral assessment. In J. D. Cone & R. P. Hawkins (Eds.), *Behavioral assessment: New directions in clinical psychology.* New York: Brunner/Mazel.

Cone, J. D., & Hawkins, R. P. (1977b). Introduction. In J. D. Cone & R. P. Hawkins (Eds.), *Behavioral assessment: New directions in clinical psychology.* New York: Brunner/Mazel.

Cone, J. D., & Haynes, S. C. (1981). *Environmental problems—behavioral solutions.* Monterey, CA: Brooks/Cole.

Cone, J. D., & Hoier, T. S. (1986). Assessing children: The radical behavioral perspective. In R. J. Prinz (Ed.), *Advances in behavioral assessment of children and families* (Vol. 2). Greenwich, CT: JAI.

Conger, A. J., Wallander, J. L., Mariotto, M. J., & Ward, D. (1980). Peer judgments of heterosexual-social anxiety and skill: What do they pay attention to anyhow? *Behavioral Assessment, 2,* 243-259.

Cook, D. T., & Campbell, D. T. (Eds.). (1979). *Quasi-experimentation: Design and analysis issues for field settings.* Chicago: Rand McNally.

Cronbach, L. J. (1957). The two disciplines of scientific psychology. *American Psychologist, 12,* 671-684.

Cronbach, L. J. (1971). Test validation. In R. L. Thorndike (Ed.), *Educational measurement* (2nd ed.). Washington, DC: American Council of Education.

Cronbach, L. J. (1972). *Fundamentos de la exploración psicológica.* Madrid: Biblioteca Nueva.

Cronbach, L. J. (1975). Beyond the two disciplines of scientific psychology. *American Psychologist, 30,* 116-127.

Cronbach, L. J. (1980). Validity on parole: How can we go straight? *New Directions for Testing and Measurement, 5,* 99-108.

Cronbach, L. J. (1982). *Designing evaluations of educational and social programs.* San Francisco: Jossey-Bass.

Cronbach, L. J. (1984a). *Essentials of psychological testing* (4th ed.). Cambridge, MA: Harper & Row.

Cronbach, L. J. (1984b). In praise of uncertainty. *Evaluation Studies Review Annual, 9,* 693-702.

Cronbach, L. J. (1988). Five perspectives on the validity argument. In H. Wainer & H. I. Braun (Eds.), *Test validity.* Hillsdale, NJ: Lawrence Erlbaum.

Cronbach, L. J. (1989). Construct validation after 30 years. In R. L. Linn (Ed.), *Intelligence: Measurement, theory, and public policy.* Urbana: University of Illinois Press.

Cronbach, L. J., & Gleser, G. (1957). *Psychological tests and personnel decisions.* Urbana: University of Illinois Press.

Cronbach, L. J., & Gleser, G. (1965). *Psychological tests and personnel decisions* (2nd ed.). Urbana: University of Illinois Press.

Cronbach, L. J., Gleser, G., Nanda, H., & Rajaratnam, N. (1972). *The dependability of behavioral measurements: Theory of generalizability for scores and profiles.* New York: John Wiley.

Cronbach, L. J., & Meehl, P. E. (1955). Construct validity in psychological tests. *Psychological Bulletin, 52,* 281-302.

Cronbach, L. J., & Quirk, T. J. (1976). Test validity. In *International encyclopedia of education.* New York: McGraw-Hill.

Cronbach, L. J., Rajaratnam, N., & Gleser, G. (1963). Theory of generalizability: A liberalization of reliability theory. *British Journal of Statistical Psychology, 16,* 137-163.

Cronbach, L. J., & Snow, R. E. (1977). *Aptitudes and instructional methods: A handbook for research on interactions.* New York: Irvington.

Cureton, E. E. (1950). Validity, reliability, and baloney. *Educational and Psychological Measurement, 10,* 94-96.

Curran, J. P. (1978). [Review of *Annual review of behavior therapy: Theory and practice* (4th ed.)]. *Behavior Modification, 2,* 135-137.

Dachener, W. (1981). Verhaltensdiagnose. Diagnose in der Verhaltenstherapie. In E. G. Wehner (Ed.), *Psychodiagnostik in Theorie und Praxis.* Frankfurt am Main: Lang.

Deitz, S. M. (1978). Current status of applied behavior analysis: Science versus technology. *American Psychologist, 33,* 805-814.

Delclaux, I., & Martínez Arias, M. R. (n.d.). *La medida en psicología.* Unpublished manuscript.

Dericco, D. A., Brigham, T. A., & Garlington, W. K. (1977). Development and evaluation of treatment paradigms for the suppression of smoking behavior. *Journal of Applied Behavior Analysis, 10,* 173-181.

Dickson, C. R. (1975). Role of assessment in behavior therapy. In P. McReynolds (Ed.), *Advances in psychological assessment* (Vol. 3). San Francisco: Jossey-Bass.

Dilthey, W. (1951). La estructura de la vida psíquica. In W. Dilthey, *Psicología y teoría del conocimiento.* Mexico City: Fondo de Cultura Económica.

Drenth, P. J. (1969). *Der psychologische Test.* Munich: Barth.

Dukes, W. F. (1965). $N = 1$. *Psychological Bulletin, 64,* 74-79.

Dumas, J. E. (1989). Let's not forget the context in behavioral assessment. *Behavioral Assessment, 11,* 231-247.

Dunnette, M. D. (1967). *Personnel selection and placement.* Belmont, CA: Wadsworth.

Embretson, S. (1983). Construct validity: Construct representation versus nomothetic span. *Psychological Bulletin, 93,* 179-197.

Emmelkamp, P. M. G. (1981). The current and future status of clinical research. *Behavioral Assessment, 3,* 249-254.

Epstein, S. (1983). Aggregation and beyond: Some basic issues in the prediction of behavior. *Journal of Personality, 51,* 360-392.

Evans, I. M. (1986). Response structure and the triple-response-mode concept. In R. O. Nelson & S. C. Hayes (Eds.), *Conceptual foundations of behavioral assessment.* New York: Guilford.

Evans, I. M., & Nelson, R. O. (1977). Assessment of child behavior problems. In A. R. Ciminero, K. S. Calhoun, & H. E. Adams (Eds.), *Handbook of behavioral assessment.* New York: John Wiley.

Evans, I. M., & Wilson, F. E. (1983). Behavioral assessment and decision making: A theoretical analysis. In M. Rozenbaum, C. M. Franks, & Y. Jaffé (Eds.), *Perspectives on behavior therapy in the eighties.* New York: Springer.

Eysenck, H. J. (1971). *Estudio científico de la personalidad.* Buenos Aires: Paidós.

Eysenck, H. J., & Rachman, S. (1965). *Causes and cures of neurosis.* London: Routledge & Kegan Paul.

Fancher, R. E. (1967). Accuracy versus validity in person perception. *Journal of Consulting Psychology, 31,* 264-269.

Fernández-Ballesteros, R. (1979). *Los métodos en evaluación conductual.* Madrid: Pablo del Río.

Fernández-Ballesteros, R. (1980). *Psicodiagnóstico. Concepto y metodologia.* Madrid: Cincel-Kapelusz.

Fernández-Ballesteros, R. (1981a). Comparaciones entre la evaluación tradicional y la evaluación conductual. In R. Fernández-Ballesteros & J. A. I. Carrobles (Eds.), *Evaluación conductual. Metodología y aplicaciones.* Madrid: Pirámide.

Fernández-Ballesteros, R. (1981b). Contenidos y modelos en evaluación conductual. In R. Fernández-Ballesteros & J. A. I. Carrobles (Eds.), *Evaluación conductual. Metodología y aplicaciones.* Madrid: Pirámide.

Fernández-Ballesteros, R. (1981c). Perspectivas históricas de la evaluación conductual. In R. Fernández-Ballesteros & J. A. I. Carrobles (Eds.), *Evaluación conductual. Metodología y aplicaciones.* Madrid: Pirámide.

Fernández-Ballesteros, R. (1983a). Los autoinformes. In R. Fernández-Ballesteros (Ed.), *Psicodiagnóstico.* Madrid: UNED.

Fernández-Ballesteros, R. (1983b). El concepto de psicodiagnóstico. In R. Fernández-Ballesteros (Ed.), *Psicodiagnóstico.* Madrid: UNED.

Fernández-Ballesteros, R. (1984). Aportaciones de la evaluación conductual a la reformulación del concepto de diagnóstico psicológico. *Anuario de Psicología, 30/31,* 31-44.

Fernández-Ballesteros, R. (1985). Evaluación psicológica y evaluación valorativa. *Evaluación Psicológica/Psychological Assessment, 1,* 7-32.

Fernández-Ballesteros, R. (1986). *Concepto integrador de la evaluación conductual.* Invited lecture at the V Congreso Latinoamericano de Análisis y Modificación del Comportamiento, Caracas, Venezuela.

Fernández-Ballesteros, R., & Carrobles, J. A. I. (Eds.). (1981a). *Evaluación conductual. Metodologia y aplicaciones.* Madrid: Pirámide.

Fernández-Ballesteros, R., & Carrobles, J. A. I. (1981b). Evaluación versus tratamiento. In R. Fernández-Ballesteros & J. A. I. Carrobles (Eds.), *Evaluación conductual. Metodología y aplicaciones.* Madrid: Pirámide.

Fernández-Ballesteros, R., & Carrobles, J. A. I. (1987). Prólogo a la tercera edición. In R. Fernández-Ballesteros & J. A. I. Carrobles (Eds.), *Evaluación conductual. Metodología y aplicaciones* (3rd ed.). Madrid: Pirámide.

Fernández-Ballesteros, R., & Maciá, A. (1983). Garantías científicas y éticas del psicodiagnóstico. In R. Fernández-Ballesteros (Ed.), *Psicodiagnóstico.* Madrid: UNED.

Fernández-Ballesteros, R., & Vizcarro, C. (1984). Problemas metodológicos en el análisis funcional de la conducta. In *Comunicaciones del I Congreso del Colegio Oficial de Psicólogos. Area 3: Psicología de la Salud.* Madrid: Colegio Oficial de Psicólogos.

Ferster, C. B. (1965). Classification of behavioral pathology. In L. Krasner & L. P. Ullmann (Eds.), *Research in behavior modification.* New York: Holt, Rinehart & Winston.

Fine, R. (1969). On the nature of scientific measure in psychology. *Psychological Reports, 24,* 519-540.

Fiske, D. W. (1971). *Measuring the concepts of personality.* Chicago: Aldine.

Fiske, D. W. (1973). Can a personality construct be validated empirically? *Psychological Bulletin, 80,* 89-92.

Fiske, D. W. (1978). *Strategies for personality research.* San Francisco: Jossey-Bass.

Fiske, D. W. (1979). Two worlds of psychological phenomena. *American Psychologist, 34,* 733-739.

Fiske, D. W. (1987). Construct invalidity comes from method effects. *Educational and Psychological Measurement, 47,* 285-307.

Fitzpatrick, A. R. (1983). The meaning of content validity. *Applied Psychological Measurement, 7,* 3-13.

Fontaine, O., & Ylieff, M. (1981). Analyse functionalle et raisonnement expérimental. *Journal de Thérapie Comportamentale, 3*, 119-130.

Ford, J. D., & Kendall, P. C. (1979). Behavior therapists' professional behaviors: Converging evidence of a gap between theory and practice. *Behavior Therapist, 2*, 37-38.

Foster, S. L., & Cone, J. D. (1980). Current issues in direct observation. *Behavioral Assessment, 2*, 313-338.

Franck, I. (1986). Psychology as a science: Resolving the idiographic-nomothetic controversy. In J. Valsiner (Ed.), *The individual subject and scientific psychology*. New York: Plenum.

Franks, C. M., & Wilson, G. T. (1978). Recent developments in behavioral assessment. In C. M. Franks & G. T. Wilson (Eds.), *Annual review of behavior therapy: Theory and practice*. New York: Brunner/Mazel.

Franks, C. M., & Wilson, G. T. (1980). Recent developments in behavioral assessment: Commentary 1979. In C. M. Franks & G. T. Wilson (Eds.), *Annual review of behavior therapy: Theory and practice*. New York: Brunner/Mazel.

Franzen, M. D. (1989). *Reliability and validity in neuropsychological assessment*. New York: Plenum.

Frederiksen, N. (1986). Construct validity and construct similarity: Methods for use in test development and test validation. *Multivariate Behavioral Research, 21*, 3-28.

Freedman, B., Rosenthal, L., Donahoe, C., Schlundt, D., & McFall, R. A. (1978). A social behavioral analysis of skills deficits in delinquent and nondelinquent adolescent boys. *Journal of Consulting and Clinical Psychology, 46*, 1448-1462.

Freeman, F. S. (1965). *Theory and practice of psychological testing*. New York: Holt, Rinehart & Winston.

Fuqua, R. W., & Schwade, J. (1986). Social validation of applied behavioral research: A selective review and critique. In A. Poling & R. W. Fuqua (Eds.), *Research methods in applied behavior analysis: Issues and advances*. New York: Plenum.

Galassi, M. D., & Galassi, J. P. (1980). Similarities and differences between two assertion measures: Factor analysis of the College Self-Expression Scale and the Rathus Assertiveness Inventory. *Behavioral Assessment, 2*, 43-57.

García Ramos, J. M. (1986). Validación de constructo en el ámbito pedagógico. *Revista Española de Pedagogía, 44*, 535-554.

Garfield, E. (1978, August). The 100 articles most cited by social scientists, 1969-1977. *Current Contents, 32*.

Ghiselli, E. E. (1955). *The measurement of occupational aptitudes*. New York: John Wiley.

Ghiselli, E. E. (1966). *The validity of occupational aptitude tests*. New York: John Wiley.

Glaser, R. (1963). Instructional technology and the measurement of learning outcomes: Some questions. *American Psychologist, 18*, 510-522.

Glaser, R., & Nitko, A. J. (1971). Measurement in learning and instruction. In R. L. Thorndike (Ed.), *Educational measurement* (2nd ed.). Washington, DC: American Council of Education.

Glass, G. V (1986). Testing old, testing new: School psychology and the allocation of intellectual resources. In B. S. Plake & J. C. Witt (Eds.), *The future of testing*. Hillsdale, NJ: Lawrence Erlbaum.

Glass, G. V, & Ellett, F. S. (1980). Evaluation research. *Annual Review of Psychology, 31*, 211-228.

Goldfried, M. R. (1977). Behavioral assessment in perspective. In J. D. Cone & R. P. Hawkins (Eds.), *Behavioral assessment: New directions in clinical psychology*. New York: Brunner/Mazel.

Goldfried, M. R. (1979). Behavioral assessment: Where do we go from here? *Behavioral Assessment, 1*, 19-22.

Goldfried, M. R. (1981). Behavioral assessment: An overview. In A. S. Bellack, M. Hersen, & A. E. Kazdin (Eds.), *International handbook of behavior modification and therapy.* New York: Plenum.

Goldfried, M. R., & Davison, G. C. (1976). *Clinical behavior therapy.* New York: Holt, Rinehart & Winston.

Goldfried, M. R., & D'Zurilla, T. J. (1969). A behavioral-analytic model for assessing competence. In C. D. Spielberger (Ed.), *Current topics in clinical and community psychology* (Vol. 1). New York: Academic Press.

Goldfried, M. R., & Kent (1972). Traditional versus behavioral personality assessment: A comparison of methodological and theoretical assumptions. *Psychological Bulletin, 77,* 409-420.

Goldfried, M. R., & Linehan, M. M. (1977). Basic issues in behavioral assessment. In A. R. Ciminero, K. S. Calhoun, & H. E. Adams (Eds.), *Handbook of behavioral assessment.* New York: John Wiley.

Goldfried, M. R., & Pomeranz, D. M. (1968). Role of assessment in behavior modification. *Psychological Reports, 23,* 75-87.

Goldfried, M. R., & Sprafkin, J. N. (1974). *Behavioral personality assessment.* Morristown, NJ: General Learning.

Goldstein, G., & Hersen, M. (1984). Historical perspectives. In G. Goldstein & M. Hersen (Eds.), *Handbook of psychological assessment.* New York: Pergamon.

Gómez Benito, J. (1986). *Los métodos causales como metología de validez de constructo.* Barcelona: Alamex.

Goodenough, F. L. (1949). *Mental testing: Its history, principles, and applications.* New York: Rinehart.

Grossmann, K. E. (1986). From idiographic approaches to nomothetic hypotheses: Stern, Allport, and the biology of knowledge, exemplified by an exploration of sibling relationships. In J. Valsiner (Ed.), *The individual subject in scientific psychology.* New York: Plenum.

Guion, R. M. (1974). Open a new window: Validities and values in psychological measurement. *American Psychologist, 29,* 287-296.

Guion, R. M. (1976). Recruiting, selection, and job placement. In M. D. Dunnette (Ed.), *Handbook of industrial and organizational psychology.* Chicago: Rand McNally.

Guion, R. M. (1977). Content validity: The source of my discontent. *Applied Psychological Measurement, 1,* 1-10.

Guion, R. M. (1980). On trinitarian doctrines of validity. *Professional Psychology, 11,* 385-398.

Haertel, E. (1985). Construct validity and criterion-referenced testing. *Review of Educational Research, 55,* 23-46.

Haney, W. (1981). Validity, vaudeville, and values: A short history of social concerns over standardized testing. *American Psychologist, 36,* 1021-1034.

Harris, J. G. (1980). Nomovalidation and idiovalidation: A quest for the true personality profile. *American Psychologist, 35,* 729-744.

Hartmann, D. P., Roper, B. L., & Bradford, D. C. (1979). Some relationships between behavioral and traditional assessment. *Journal of Behavioral Assessment, 1,* 3-21.

Hattie, J. (1985). Methodology review: Assessing unidimensionality of tests and items. *Applied Psychological Measurement, 9,* 139-164.

Hawkins, R. P. (1975). Who decided that was the problem? Two stages of responsibility for applied behavior analysts. In W. S. Wood (Ed.), *Issues in evaluating behavior modification.* Champaign, IL: Research Press.

Hawkins, R. P. (1986). Selection of target behaviors. In R. O. Nelson & S. C. Hayes (Eds.), *Conceptual foundations of behavioral assessment.* New York: Guilford.

Hay, W. M., Hay, L. R., & Nelson, R. O. (1977). Direct and collateral changes in on-task and academic behavior resulting from on-task versus academic contingencies. *Behavior Therapy, 8,* 431-441.

Hayes, S. C., & Cavior, N. (1980). Multiple tracking and the reactivity of self-monitoring: II. Positive behaviors. *Behavioral Assessment, 2,* 283-296.

Hayes, S. C., & Nelson, R. O. (1986). Assessing the effects of therapeutic interventions. In R. O. Nelson & S. C. Hayes (Eds.), *Conceptual foundations of behavioral assessment.* New York: Guilford.

Hayes, S. C., Nelson, R. O., & Jarrett, R. B. (1986). Evaluating the quality of behavioral assessment. In R. O. Nelson & S. C. Hayes (Eds.), *Conceptual foundations of behavioral assessment.* New York: Guilford.

Hayes, S. C., Nelson, R. O., & Jarrett, R. B. (1987). The treatment utility of assessment: A functional approach to evaluating assessment quality. *American Psychologist, 42,* 963-974.

Haynes, S. N. (1978). *Principles of behavioral assessment.* New York: Gardner.

Haynes, S. N. (1979). Behavioral variance, individual differences and trait theory in a behavioral construct system: A reappraisal. *Behavioral Assessment, 1,* 41-49.

Haynes, S. N. (1983). Behavioral assessment. In M. Hersen, A. E. Kazdin, & A. S. Bellack (Eds.), *The clinical psychology handbook.* New York: Pergamon.

Haynes, S. N. (1986). The design of intervention programs. In R. O. Nelson & S. C. Hayes (Eds.), *Conceptual foundations of behavioral assessment.* New York: Guilford.

Haynes, S. N. (1988). Causal models and the assessment-treatment relationship in behavior therapy. *Journal of Psychopathology and Behavioral Assessment, 10,* 171-183.

Haynes, S. N. (1990). Behavioral assessment of adults. In G. Goldstein & M. Hersen (Eds.), *Handbook of psychological assessment* (2nd ed.). Boston: Allyn & Bacon.

Haynes, S. N. (1991). Behavioral assessment. In M. Hersen, A. E. Kazdin, & A. S. Bellack (Eds.), *The clinical psychology handbook* (2nd ed.). Boston: Allyn & Bacon.

Haynes, S. N., Follingstad, D. R., & Sullivan, J. (1979). Asssment of marital satisfaction and interaction. *Journal of Consulting and Clinical Psychology, 47,* 789-791.

Haynes, S. N., & Horn, W, F. (1982). Reactive effects of behavioral observation. *Behavioral Assessment, 4,* 443-469.

Haynes, S. N., Jensen, B. J., Wise, E., & Sherman, D. (1981). The marital intake interview: A multimethod criterion validity assessment. *Journal of Consulting and Clinical Psychology, 49,* 379-387.

Haynes, S. N., & O'Brien, W. H. (1988). The Gordian knot of DSM-III-R use: Integrating principles of behavior classification and complex causal models. *Behavioral Assessment, 10,* 95-105.

Haynes, S. N., & Wilson, C. C. (1979). *Behavioral assessment.* San Francisco: Jossey-Bass.

Henson, D. E., Rubinm, H. B., & Henson, C. (1979), Consistency of the labial temperature change measure of human female heroticism. *Behavior Research and Therapy, 17,* 226-240.

Hersen, M. (1976). Historical perspectives in behavioral assessment. In M. Hersen & A. S. Bellack (Eds.), *Behavioral assessment: A practical handbook.* New York: Pergamon.

Hersen, M. (1988). Behavioral assessment and psychiatric diagnosis. *Behavioral Assessment, 10,* 107-121.

Hersen, M., & Barlow, D. H. (1976). *Single case experimental designs: Strategies for studying behavior change.* New York: Pergamon.

Hersen, M., & Bellack, A. S. (Eds.). (1988a). *Dictionary of behavioral assessment techniques.* New York: Pergamon.

Hersen, M., & Bellack, A. S. (1988b). DSM-III and behavioral assessment. In A. S. Bellack & M. Hersen (Eds.), *Behavioral assessment: A practical handbook* (3rd ed.). New York: Pergamon.

Hoermann, H. (1964). *Aussagemoeglichkeiten psychologischer Diagnostik.* Göttingen: Hogrefe.

Hogan, R., & Nicholson, R. A. (1988). The meaning of personality test scores. *American Psychologist, 43,* 621-626.

Holt, R. R. (1984). Freud, the free will controversy, and prediction in personology. In R. A. Zucker, J. Aronoff, & A. I. Rabin (Eds.), *Personality and the prediction of behavior.* New York: Academic Press.

Huber, H. P. (1973). *Psychometrische Einzelfalldiagnostik.* Weinheim: Beltz.

Jackson, D. N., & Paunonen, S. V. (1980). Personality structure and assessment. *Annual Review of Psychology, 31,* 503-551.

Johnson, S. M., & Bolstad, O. D. (1973). Methodological issues in naturalistic observation: Some problems and solutions for field research. In L. A. Hamerlynck, L. C. Handy, & E. J. Mash (Eds.), *Behavior change: Methodology, concepts, and practice.* Champaign, IL: Research Press.

Johnson, W. (1946). *People in quandries.* New York: Harper & Row.

Johnston, J. M., & Pennypacker, H. S. (1980). *Strategies and tactics of human behavioral research.* Hillsdale, NJ: Lawrence Erlbaum.

Jones, E. E., & Nisbett, R. (1972). The actor and the observer: Divergent perceptions of the causes of behavior. In E. E. Jones et al. (Eds.), *Attribution: Perceiving the causes of behavior.* Morristown, NJ: General Learning.

Jones, R. (1983). Functional analysis: Some cautionary notes. *Bulletin of the British Psychological Society, 36,* 237-238.

Jones, R. R. (1973). Behavioral observation and frequency data: Problems in scoring, analysis, and interpretation. In L. A. Hamerlynck, L. C. Handy, & E. J. Mash (Eds.), *Behavior change: Methodology, concepts, and practice.* Champaign, IL: Research Press.

Jones, R. R. (1977). Conceptual versus analytic uses of generalizability theory in behavioral assessment. In J. D. Cone & R. P. Hawkins (Eds.), *Behavioral assessment: New directions in clinical psychology.* New York: Brunner/Mazel.

Kagan, J. (1988). The meanings of personality predicates. *American Psychologist, 43,* 614-620.

Kane, M. T. (1982). A sampling model for validity. *Applied Psychological Measurement, 6,* 125-160.

Kanfer, F. H. (1972). Assessment for behavior modification. *Journal of Personality Assessment, 36,* 418-423.

Kanfer, F. H. (1979). A few comments on the current status of behavioral assessment. *Behavioral Assessment, 1,* 37-39.

Kanfer, F. H., & Busemayer, J. R. (1982). The use of problem solving and decision making in behavior therapy. *Clinical Psychology Review, 2,* 239-266.

Kanfer, F. H., & Nay, W. R. (1982). Behavioral assessment. In G. T. Wilson & C. M. Franks (Eds.), *Contemporary behavior therapy.* New York: Guilford.

Kanfer, F. H., & Saslow, G. (1965). Behavioral analysis. *Archives of General Psychiatry, 12,* 529-538.

Kanfer, F. H., & Saslow, G. (1969). Behavioral diagnosis. In C. M. Franks (Ed.), *Behavior therapy: Appraisal and status.* New York: McGraw-Hill.

Kaplan, A. (1964). *The conduct of inquiry: Methodology for behavioral science.* San Francisco: Chandler.

Kazdin, A. E. (1977a). Artifact, bias, and complexity of assessment: The ABCs of reliability. *Journal of Applied Behavior Analysis, 10,* 141-150.

Kazdin, A. E. (1977b). Assessing the clinical or applied importance of behavior change through social validation. *Behavior Modification, 1,* 427-452.

Kazdin, A. E. (1982). *Single-case research designs: Methods for clinical and applied settings.* New York: Oxford University Press.

Kazdin, A. E. (1983). Pyschiatric diagnosis, dimensions of dysfunction, and child behavior therapy. *Behavior Therapy, 14,* 73-99.

Kazdin, A. E. (1985). Selection of target behaviors: The relationship of the treatment focus to clinical dysfunction. *Behavioral Assessment, 7,* 33-47.

Kelly, G. A. (1955). *The psychology of personal constructs.* New York: W. W. Norton.

Kendall, P. C. (1984). Behavioral assessment and methodology. In C. M. Franks & G. T. Wilson (Eds.), *Annual review of behavior therapy: Theory and practice* (Vol. 9). New York: Guilford.

Kendall, P. C. (1985). Behavioral assessment and methodology. In C. M. Franks, G. T. Wilson, P. C. Kendall, & K. D. Brownell (Eds.), *Annual review of behavior therapy: Theory and practice* (Vol. 10). New York: Guilford.

Kendall, P. C., & Hollon, S. D. (Eds.). (1981). *Assessment strategies for cognitive-behavioral interventions.* New York: Academic Press.

Kerlinger, F. N. (1973). *Foundations of behavioral research.* New York: Holt, Rinehart & Winston.

Klauer, K. J. (1984). Kontentvalidität. *Diagnostica, 30,* 1-23.

Kleinmuntz, B. (1967). *Personality measurement: An introduction.* Homewood, IL: Dorsey.

Korchin, S. J., & Schuldberg, D. (1981). The future of clinical assessment. *American Psychologist, 36,* 1147-1158.

Kratochwill, T. R. (Ed.). (1978). *Single subject research: Strategies for evaluating change.* New York: Academic Press.

Kratochwill, T. R. (1985). Selection of target behaviors in behavioral consultation. *Behavioral Assessment, 7,* 49-61.

Kroger, R. O. (1968). Conceptual and empirical independence in test validation: A note on Campbell and Fiske's "discriminant validity." *Educational and Psychological Measurement, 28,* 383-387.

Kurtz, A. K. (1948). A research test of the Rorschach test. *Personnel Psychology, 1,* 41-51.

Lahey, B. B., Vosk, B. N., & Habif, V. L. (1981). Behavioral assessment of learning disabled children: A rationale and strategy. *Behavioral Assessment, 3,* 3-14.

Lamiell, J. T. (1981). Toward an idiothetic psychology of personality. *American Psychologist, 36,* 276-289.

Lamiell, J. T. (1982). The case for an idiothetic psychology of personality: A conceptual and empirical foundation. In B. Maher (Ed.), *Progress in experimental personality research* (Vol. 11). New York: Academic Press.

Lamiell, J. T. (1987). *The psychology of personality: An epistemological inquiry.* New York: Columbia University Press.

Lamiell, J. T., Foss, M. A., Larsen, R. J., & Hempel, A. M. (1983). Studies in intuitive personology from an idiothetic point of view: Implications for personality theory. *Journal of Personality, 51,* 438-467.

Lamiell, J. T., & Trierweiler, S. J. (1986). Personality measurement and intuitive personality judgements from an idiothetic point of view. *Clinical Psychology Review, 6,* 471-491.

Lamiell, J. T., Trierweiler, S. J., & Foss, M. A. (1983). Detecting (in)consistencies in personality: Reconciling intuitions and empirical evidence. *Journal of Personality Assessment, 47,* 380-389.

Landau, R. J., & Goldfried, M. R. (1981). The assessment of schemata: A unifying framework for cognitive, behavioral, and traditional assessment. In P. C. Kendall & S. D. Hollon (Eds.), *Assessment strategies for cognitive-behavioral interventions.* New York: Academic Press.

Landorf, P. (1976). Krise der Diagnostik (Fortsetzung der Diskussion). *Zeitschrift für Psychologie, 35,* 49-61.

Landorf, P. (1978). Die Validierung des Diagnostikers. In U. Pulver, A. Lang, & F. Schmid (Eds.), *Ist Psychodiagnostik verantwortbar?* Bern: Huber.

Landy, F. J. (1986). Stamp collecting versus science: Validation as hypothesis testing. *American Psychologist, 41,* 1183-1192.

Lang, A. (1978a). Einige Überlegungen zur Rechtfertigung psychodiagnostischer Tätigkeit in der Beratung. In U. Pulver, A. Lang, & F. Schmid (Eds.), *Ist Psychodiagnostik verantwortbar?* Bern: Huber.

Lang, A. (1978b). Das Problem mit der Psychodiagnostik: Kein gutes Fundament für eine Profession! In U. Pulver, A. Lang, & F. Schmid (Eds.), *Ist Psychodiagnostik verantwortbar?* Bern: Huber.

Lanyon, R. I. (1984). Personality assessment. *Annual Review of Psychology, 35,* 667-701.

Lanyon, R. I., & Lanyon, B. J. (1976). Behavioral assessment and decision making: The design of strategies for therapeutic behavior change. In M. P. Feldmann & A. Broadhurst (Eds.), *Theoretical and experimental bases of the behavior therapies.* London: John Wiley.

Leitenberg, H. (1978). [Review of *Behavioral assessment: A practical handbook*]. *Behavior Modification, 2,* 137-139.

Lennon, R. T. (1956). Assumptions underlying the use of content validity. *Educational and Psychological Measurement, 16,* 294-304.

Levy, P. (1973). On the relation between test theory and psychology. In P. Kline (Ed.), *New approaches in psychological measurement.* London: John Wiley.

Lewin, K. (1973). *Dinámica de la Personalidad.* Madrid: Morata.

Linehan, M. M. (1980). Content validity: Its relevance to behavioral assessment. *Behavioral Assessment, 2,* 147-159.

Livingston, S. A. (1977). Psychometric techniques for criterion-referenced testing and behavioral assessment. In J. D. Cone & R. P. Hawkins (Eds.), *Behavioral assessment: New directions in clinical psychology.* New York: Brunner/Mazel.

Llavona, L. (1984). El proceso de evaluación conductual. In J. Mayor & F. J. Labrador (Eds.), *Manual de modificación de conducta.* Madrid: Alhambra.

Loevinger, J. (1957). Objective tests as instruments of psychological theory. *Psychological Reports, Monograph 9,* 635-694.

Loevinger, J. (1959). Theory and techniques of assessment. *Annual Review of Psychology, 10,* 289-316.

Loevinger, J. (1965). Person and population as psychometric concepts. *Psychological Review, 72,* 143-155.

Lord, R. G. (1985). Accuracy in behavioral measurement: An alternative definition based on raters' cognitive schema and signal detection theory. *Journal of Applied Psychology, 70,* 66-71.

Lumsden, J. (1976). Test theory. *Annual Review of Psychology, 27,* 251-280.

Manicas, P., & Secord, P. F. (1983). Implications for psychology of the new philosophy of science. *American Psychologist, 38,* 399-413.

Marceil, J. C. (1977). Implicit dimensions of idiography and nomothesis: A reformulation. *American Psychologist, 32,* 1046-1055.

March, A. (1957). *Das neue Denken der modernen Physik.* Hamburg.

Martens, K. B., & Witt, J. C. (1988). Ecological behavior analysis. In M. Hersen, R. M. Eisler, & P. M. Miller (Eds.), *Progress in behavior modification* (Vol. 22). Newbury Park, CA: Sage.

Martin, P., & Bateson, P. (1987). *Measuring behavior: An introductory guide.* Cambridge, MA: Cambridge University Press.

Martínez Arias, M. R. (1981). Principios psicométricos de las técnicas en evaluación conductual. In R. Fernández-Ballesteros & J. A. I. Carrobles (Eds.), *Evaluación conductual.
Metodología y aplicaciones*. Madrid: Pirámide.

Mash, E. J. (1979). What is behavioral assessment? *Behavioral Assessment, 1,* 23-29.

Mash, E. J. (1985). Some comments on target selection in behavior therapy. *Behavioral
Assessment, 7,* 63-78.

Mash, E. J., & Terdal, L. G. (1974). Behavior therapy assessment: Diagnosis, design, and
evaluation. *Psychological Reports, 35,* 587-601.

Mash, E. J., & Terdal, L. G. (1981). Behavioral assessment of childhood disturbance. In E.
J. Mash & L. G. Terdal (Eds.), *Behavioral assessment of childhood disorders*. New York:
Guilford.

Matesanz, A. (1975). La validez como criterio valorativo de las medidas psicológicas. *Revista
de Psicología General y Aplicada, 30,* 871-902.

May, E. (1955). Zur erkenntnistheoretischen Problematik der wissenschaftlichen Psychologie. In A. Wellek (Ed.), *20. Kongress der Deutschen Gesellschaft für Psychologie,
Berlin, 1955*. Göttingen: Hogrefe.

McClelland, D. C. (1981). Is personality consistent? In A. I. Rabin et al. (Eds.), *Further
explorations in personality*. New York: John Wiley.

McFall, R. M. (1982). A review and reformulation of the concept of social skills. *Behavioral
Assessment, 4,* 1-33.

McFall, R. M. (1986). Theory and method in assessment: The vital link. *Behavioral Assessment, 8,* 3-10.

McGlynn, F. D., McNeil, D. W., Gallagher, S. L., & Vrana, S. (1987). Factor structure,
stability, and internal consistency of the Dental Fear Survey. *Behavioral Assessment, 9,*
57-66.

McReynolds, P. (1971). Introduction. In P. McReynolds (Ed.), *Advances in psychological
assessment* (Vol. 2). Palo Alto, CA: Science & Behavior.

McReynolds, P. (1977). Introduction. In P. McReynolds (Ed.), *Advances in psychological
assessment* (Vol. 4). San Francisco: Jossey-Bass.

McReynolds, P. (1985). Psychological assessment and clinical practice: Problems and prospects. In J. N. Butcher & C. D. Spielberger (Eds.), *Advances in personality assessment*
(Vol. 4). Hillsdale, NJ: Lawrence Erlbaum.

McReynolds, P. (1986). History of assessment in clinical and educational settings. In R. O.
Nelson & S. C. Hayes (Eds.), *Conceptual foundations of behavioral assessment*. New
York: Guilford.

Meehl, P. E. (1954). *Clinical versus statistical prediction. A theoretical analysis and a review
of the evidence*. Minneapolis: University of Minnesota Press.

Meehl, P. E. (1957). When shall we use our heads instead of the formula? *Journal of
Counseling Psychology, 4,* 268-273.

Meehl, P. E. (1971). The cognitive activity of the clinician. In L. D. Goodstein & R. I. Lanyon
(Eds.), *Readings in personality assessment*. New York: John Wiley. (Original work
published 1960)

Meehl, P. E. (1973a). Some ruminations on the validation of clinical procedures. In P. E.
Meehl, *Psychodiagnosis: Selected papers*. London: Oxford University Press. (Original
work published 1959)

Meehl, P. E. (1973b). Why I do not attend case conferences. In P. E. Meehl, *Psychodiagnosis:
Selected papers*. London: Oxford University Press.

Meehl, P. E. (1978). Theoretical risks and tabular asterisks: Sir Karl, Sir Ronald, and the slow
progress of soft psychology. *Journal of Consulting and Clinical Psychology, 46,* 806-834.

Meehl, P. E. (1979). A funny thing happened to us on the way to the latent entities. *Journal
of Personality Assessment, 43,* 564-577.

Meehl, P. E., & Rosen, A. (1955). Antecedent probability and efficiency of psychometric signs, patterns or cutting scores. *Psychological Bulletin, 52,* 194-216.

Merz, F. (1966). Prognose und Bewährung: Grundlegende Probleme. In K. Holzkamp, A. O. Jaeger, & F. Merz (Eds.), *Prognose und Bewährung in der Psychologischen Diagnostik.* Göttingen: Hogrefe.

Messick, S. (1975). The standard problem: Meanings and values in measurement and evaluation. *American Psychologist, 30,* 955-966.

Messick, S. (1980). Test validity and the ethics of assessment. *American Psychologist, 35,* 1012-1027.

Messick, S. (1981a). Constructs and their vicissitudes in educational and psychological measurement. *Psychological Bulletin, 89,* 575-588.

Messick, S. (1981b, November). Evidence and ethics in the evaluation of tests. *Educational Researcher,* pp. 9-20.

Messick, S. (1988). The once and future issues of validity: Assessing the meaning and consequences of measurement. In H. Wainer & H. I. Braun (Eds.), *Test validity.* Hillsdale, NJ: Lawrence Erlbaum.

Messick, S. (1989). Validity. In R. L. Linn (Ed.), *Educational measurement* (3rd ed.). New York: American Council of Education, Macmillan, & Collier Macmillan.

Meyer, V., & Chesser, E. (1970). *Behaviour therapy in clinical psychiatry.* Harmondsworth, UK: Penguin.

Michel, L., & Mai, N. (1968). Entscheidungstheorie und Probleme der Diagnostik bei Cronbach und Gleser. *Diagnostica, 14,* 109-120.

Mischel, W. (1968). *Personality and assessment.* New York: John Wiley.

Mischel, W. (1972). Direct versus indirect personality assessment: Evidence and implications. *Journal of Consulting and Clinical Psychology, 40,* 319-324.

Mischel, W. (1983). Alternatives in the pursuit of the predictability and consistency of persons: Stable data that yield unstable interpretations. *Journal of Personality, 51,* 578-604.

Mischel, W. (1984a). Convergences and challenges in the search for consistency. *American Psychologist, 39,* 351-364.

Mischel, W. (1984b). On the predictability of behavior and the structure of personality. In R. A. Zucker, J. Aronoff, & A. I. Rabin (Eds.), *Personality and the prediction of behavior.* New York: Academic Press.

Mischel, W. (1985). Assessment from a cognitive social learning perspective. *Evaluación Psicológica/Psychological Assessment, 1,* 33-58.

Mischel, W. (1988). [Review of Nelson, R. O., & Hayes, S. C. (Eds.), *Conceptual foundations of behavioral assessment*]. *Behavioral Assessment, 10,* 125-128.

Mitroff, I. I., & Sagasti, F. (1973). Epistemology as general systems theory: An approach to the design of complex decision-making experiments. *Philosophy of Social Science, 3,* 117-134.

Monroe, W. (1937). *Some trends in educational measurement.* In the Twenty-Fourth Annual Conference on Educational Measurement. Bloomington: University of Indiana Press.

Morales, P. (1988). *Medición de actitudes en psicología y educación. Constucción de escalas y problemas metodológicos.* San Sebastián: Ttarttalo.

Mullini, S. D., & Galassi, J. P. (1981). Deriving the content of social skills training with a verbal response components approach. *Behavioral Assessment, 3,* 55-66.

Musso, J. R. (1970). *Falacias y mitos metodológicos de la psicología.* Buenos Aires: Psiqué.

Nathan, P. E. (1981). Symptomatic diagnosis and behavioral assessment: A synthesis. In D. H. Barlow (Ed.), *Behavioral assessment of adult disorders.* New York: Guilford.

Nelson, R. O. (1981). Realistic dependent measures for clinical use. *Journal of Consulting and Clinical Psychology, 49,* 168-182.

Nelson, R. O. (1983a). Behavioral assessment: Past, present, and future. *Behavioral Assessment, 5,* 195-206.

Nelson, R. O. (1983b). Current status and new developments in behavioral assessment. In A. E. Kazdin (Chair), *Behavioral assessment: Historical development, advances, and current status.* Symposium conducted at the meeting of the Association for the Advancement of Behavior Therapy, Washington, DC.

Nelson, R. O. (1987). DSM-III and behavioral assessment. In C. G. Last & M. Hersen (Eds.), *Issues in diagnostic research.* New York: Plenum.

Nelson, R. O. (1988). Relationship between assessment and treatment within a behavioral perspective. *Journal of Psychopathology and Behavioral Assessment, 10,* 155-170.

Nelson, R. O., & Barlow, D. H. (1981). An overview of behavioral assessment with adult clients: Basic strategies and initial procedures. In D. H. Barlow (Ed.), *Behavioral assessment of adult disorders.* New York: Guilford.

Nelson, R. O., Hay, L. R., & Hay, W. M. (1977). Comment on Cone's "The relevance of reliability and validity for behavior assessment." *Behavior Therapy, 8,* 427-430.

Nelson, R. O., & Hayes, S. C. (1979a). The nature of behavioral assessment: A commentary. *Journal of Applied Behavioral Analysis, 12,* 491-500.

Nelson, R. O., & Hayes, S. C. (1979b). Some current dimensions of behavioral assessment. *Behavioral Assessment, 1,* 1-16.

Nelson, R. O., & Hayes, S. C. (1981). Nature of behavioral assessment. In M. Hersen & A. S. Bellack (Eds), *Behavioral assessment: A practical handbook* (2nd ed.). New York: Pergamon.

Nelson, R. O., & Hayes, S. C. (Eds.). (1986a). *Conceptual foundations of behavioral assessment.* New York: Guilford.

Nelson, R. O., & Hayes, S. C. (1986b). The nature of behavioral assessment. In R. O. Nelson & S. C. Hayes (Eds.), *Conceptual foundations of behavioral assessment.* New York: Guilford.

Nelson, R. O., & Hayes, S. C. (n.d.). *Behavioral assessment: Creating a comprehensive alternative to traditional assessment approaches.* Unpublished manuscript.

Nelson, R. O., & Maser, J. D. (1988). The DSM and depression: Potential contributions of behavioral assessment. *Behavioral Assessment, 10,* 45-65.

Nitko, A. J. (1984). Defining "criterion-referenced test." In R. A. Berk (Ed.), *A guide to criterion-referenced test construction.* Baltimore, MD: Johns Hopkins University Press.

Novick, R. M. (1984). Importance of professional standards for fair and appropriate test use. In C. W. Davies (Ed.), *The uses and misuses of tests.* San Francisco: Jossey-Bass.

Nunnally, J. C. (1978). *Psychometric theory.* New York: McGraw-Hill.

Nunnally, J. C., & Durham, R. L. (1975). Validity, reliability, and special problems of measurement in evaluation research. In E. L. Struening & M. Guttentag (Eds.), *Handbook of evaluation research* (Vol. 1). London: Sage.

Office of Strategic Services. (1948). *Assessment of men.* New York: Holt, Rinehart & Winston.

O'Leary, K. D. (1979). Behavioral assessment. *Behavioral Assessment, 1,* 31-36.

Ollendick, T. H. (1983). Reliability and validity of the Revised Fear Survey Schedule for Children. *Behavior Research and Therapy, 21,* 685-692.

Owens, R. G., & Ashcroft, J. B. (1982). Functional analysis in applied psychology. *British Journal of Clinical Psychology, 21,* 181-189.

Ozer, D. J. (1989). Construct validity in personality assessment. In D. M. Buss & N. Cantor (Eds.), *Personality psychology: Recent trends and emerging directions.* New York: Springer.

Pap, A. (1953). Reduction-sentences and open concepts. *Methods, 5,* 3-30.

Patterson, G. R., & Bank, L. (1986). Bootstrapping your way in the nomological thicket. *Behavioral Assessment, 8,* 49-73.

Paunonen, S. V. (1984). Optimizing the validity of personality assessments: The importance of aggregation and item content. *Journal of Research in Personality, 18,* 411-431.

Pawlik, K. (1976). Modell- und Praxisdimensionen psychologischer Diagnostik. In K. Pawlik (Ed.), *Diagnose der Diagnostik.* Stuttgart: Klett.

Pervin, L. A. (1984). Idiographic approaches to personality. In N. S. Endler & J. M. Hunt (Eds.), *Personality and the behavioral disorders.* New York: John Wiley.

Peterson, D. R. (1968). *The clinical study of social behavior.* New York: Appleton-Century-Crofts.

Plaum, E. (1982). Wissenschaftliche fundierte klinisch-psychologische Diagnostik—Ein Qualitätsmerkmal moderner Psychotherapie. *Report Psychologie, 7,* 5-6.

Plessen, U. (1981). Möglichkeiten einer therapiezielorietierten Einzelfalldiagnostik. In H. Bommert & M. Hockel (Eds.), *Therapie orientierte Diagnostik.* Stuttgart: Kohlhammer.

Popham, W. J. (1978). *Criterion-referenced measurement.* Englewood Cliffs, NJ: Prentice-Hall.

Prieto, F., Tortosa, F., & Silva, F. (1984). *La evaluación conductual: aproximación bibliométrica.* Paper presented at the I Congreso de Evaluación Psicológica, Madrid

Primoff, E. S. (1952). Job analysis tests to rescue trade testing from make-believe and shrinkage. *American Psychologist, 7,* 486 (Abstract).

Prout, H. T. (1986). Personality assessment and individual therapeutic interventions. In H. M. Knoff (Ed.), *The assessment of child and adolescent personality.* New York: Guilford.

Pulver, U. (1978a). Die Krise der psychologischen Diagnostik—Eine Koartationskrise. In U. Pulver, A. Lang, & F. Schmid (Eds.), *Ist Psychodiagnostik verantwortbar?* Bern: Huber.

Pulver, U. (1978b). Von der Mannigfaltigkeit psychologischer Erfassungsmittel in der Baratung. In U. Pulver, A. Lang, & F. Schmid (Eds.), *Ist Psychodiagnostik verantwortbar?* Bern: Huber.

Pulver, U., Lang, A., & Schmid, F. (Eds.). (1978). *Ist Psychodiagnostik verantwortbar?* Bern: Huber.

Raven, J. C. (1966). *Psychological principles appropriate to social and clinical problems.* London: Lewis.

Raven, J. C. (1989). Questionable assumptions in test construction. *Bulletin of the International Test Commission, 28/29,* 67-95.

Reichenbach, H. (1938). *Experience and prediction.* Chicago: University of Chicago Press.

Repp, A. C., et al. (1989). Conducting behavioral assessments on computer-collected data. *Behavioral Assessment, 11,* 249-268.

Robin, A. C., & Weiss, J. G. (1980). Criterion-related validity of behavioral self-report measures of problem solving communication skills in distresses and non-distressed parent-adolescent dyads. *Behavioral Assessment, 2,* 339-352.

Rogers-Warren, A., & Warren, S. F. (Eds.). (1977). *Ecological perspectives in behavior analysis.* Baltimore: University Park Press.

Rorer, L. G., & Widiger, T. A. (1983). Personality structure and assessment. *Annual Review of Psychology, 34,* 431-463.

Rubin, D. B. (1988). Discussion. In H. Wainer & H. I. Braun (Eds.), *Test validity.* Hillsdale, NJ: Lawrence Erlbaum.

Runyan, W. M. (1983). Idiographic goals and methods in the study of lives. *Journal of Personality, 51,* 413-437.

Russo, D. C., Bird, B. L., & Masek, B. J. (1980). Assessment issues in behavioral medicine. *Behavioral Assessment, 2,* 1-18.

Rust, J., & Golombok, S. (1989). *Modern psychometrics: The science of psychological assessment.* London: Routledge.

Schaarschmidt, U. (1984). Tasks and prospects of psychodiagnostics in the GDR. *Newsletter of the International Test Commission, 19,* 3-23.

Schaller, S., & Schmidtke, A. (1983). Verhaltensdiagnostik. In K. J. Groffmann & L. Michel (Eds.), *Verhaltensdiagnostik (Enzyklopaedie der Psychologie, BII, 4).* Göttingen: Hogrefe.

Schoenfeldt, L. F. (1984). The status of test validation research. In B. S. Plake (Ed.), *Social and technical issues in testing* (Vol. 1). Hillsdale, NJ: Lawrence Erlbaum.

Schulte, D. (1973). Der diagnostische-therapeutische Prozess in der Verhaltenstherapie. In J. C. Brengelmann & W. Tunner (Eds.), *Behavior therapy—Verhaltenstherapie.* Munich: Urban & Schwarzenberg.

Schulte, D. (Ed.). (1974). *Diagnostik in der Verhaltenstherapie.* Munich: Urban & Schwarzenberg.

Schulte, D. (1976). Psychodiagnostik zur Erklärung und Modifikation von Verhalten. In K. Pawlik (Ed.), *Diagnose der Diagnostik.* Stuttgart: Klett.

Schulte, D., & Wittchen, H. U. (1988). Wert und Nutzen klassifikatorischer Diagnostik für die Psychotherapie. *Diagnostica, 34,* 85-98.

Sechrest, L. (1963). Incremental validity: A recommendation. *Educational and Psychological Measurement, 23,* 153-158.

Shadish, W. R. (1986). Planned critical multiplism: Some elaborations. *Behavioral Assessment, 8,* 75-103.

Shapiro, M. B. (1961a). A method of measuring psychological changes specific to the individual psychiatric patient. *British Journal of Medical Psychology, 34,* 151-155.

Shapiro, M. B. (1961b). The single case in fundamental clinical psychology research. *British Journal of Medical Psychology, 34,* 255-263.

Shapiro, M. B. (1964). The measurement of clinically relevant variables. *Journal of Psychosomatic Research, 8,* 245-254.

Shapiro, M. B. (1970). Intensive assessment of the single case: An inductive-deductive approach. In P. Mittler (Ed.), *The psychological assessment of mental and physical handicaps.* London: Methuen.

Shapiro, M. B. (1985). A reassessment of clinical psychology as an applied science. *British Journal of Clinical Psychology, 24,* 1-11.

Shavelson, R. J., Webb, N. M., & Rowley, G. L. (1989). Generalizability theory. *American Psychologist, 44,* 922-932.

Sidman, M. (1960). *Tactics of scientific research.* New York: Basic Books.

Silva, F. (1978). El análisis funcional de conducta como disciplina diagnóstica. *Análisis y Modificación de Conducta, 4,* 28-55.

Silva, F. (1980). Análisis funcional de conducta y diagnóstico psicológico. *Análisis y Modificación de Conducta, 6,* 347-352.

Silva, F. (1982). *Introducción al psicodiagnóstico.* Valencia: Promolibro.

Silva, F. (1984). *Psicodiagnóstico: teoría y aplicación.* Valencia: Centro Editorial de Servicios y Publicaciones Universitarias.

Silva, F. (1988). La evaluación psicológica como proceso. *Evaluación Psicológica/Psychological Assessment, 4,* 31-50.

Sines, L. K. (1971). The relative contributions of four kinds of data to accuracy in personality assessment. In L. D. Goodstein & R. I. Lanyon (Eds.), *Readings in personality assessment.* New York: John Wiley. (Original work published 1959)

Skinner, B. F. (1938). *The behavior of organisms.* New York: Appleton-Century-Crofts.

Skinner, B. F. (1953). *Science and human behavior.* New York: Macmillan.

Staats, A. W. (1975). *Social behaviorism.* Homewood, IL: Dorsey.

Staats, A. W. (1980). Behavioural interaction and interactional psychology theories of personality: Similarities, differences and the need for unification. *British Journal of Psychology, 71,* 205-220.

Staats, A. W. (1986). Behaviorism with a personality: The paradigmatic behavioral assessment approach. In R. O. Nelson & S. C. Hayes (Eds.), *Conceptual foundations of behavioral assessment.* New York: Guilford.

Staats, A. W., & Fernández-Ballesteros, R. (1987). The self-report in personality measurement: A paradigmatic behaviorism approach to psychodiagnostics. *Evaluación Psicológica/Psychological Assessment, 3,* 151-189.

Staats, A. W., & Fernández-Ballesteros, R. (1988). *Paradigmatic behavioral assessment.* Unpublished manuscript.

Staats, A. W., & Staats, C. K. (1963). *Complex human behavior.* New York: Holt, Rinehart & Winston.

Strosahl, K. D., & Linehan, M. M. (1986). Basic issues in behavioral assessment. In A. R. Ciminero, K. S. Calhoun, & H. E. Adams (Eds.), *Handbook of behavioral assessment* (2nd ed.). New York: John Wiley.

Strossen, R. J., Coates, T. J., & Thoresen, C. E. (1979). Extending generalizability theory to single-subject designs. *Behavior Therapy, 10,* 606-614.

Suen, H. K. (1988). Agreement, reliability, accuracy, and validity: Toward a clarification. *Behavioral Assessment, 10,* 343-366.

Suen, H. K., & Ary, D. (1989). *Analyzing quantitative behavioral observation data.* Hillsdale, NJ: Lawrence Erlbaum.

Sundberg, N. D. (1977). *Assessment of persons.* Englewood Cliffs, NJ: Prentice-Hall.

Sundberg, N. D., & Tyler, L. E. (1962). *Clinical psychology: An introduction to research and practice.* New York: Appleton-Century-Crofts.

Sundberg, N. D., Tyler, L. E., & Taplin, J. R. (1973). *Clinical psychology: Expanding horizons.* Englewood Cliffs, NJ: Prentice-Hall.

Swan, G. E., & MacDonald, M. L. (1978). Behavior therapy in practice: A national survey of behavior therapists. *Behavior Therapy, 9,* 799-807.

Taft, R. (1971). Multiple methods of personality assessment. In L. D. Goodstein & R. I. Lanyon (Eds.), *Readings in personality assessment.* New York: John Wiley. (Original work published 1959)

Tallent, N. (1965). Clinical psychological testing: A review of premises, practices and promises. *Journal of Projective Techniques and Personality Assessment, 29,* 418-435.

Taylor, C. B. (1983). DSM-III and behavioral assessment. *Behavioral Assessment, 5,* 5-14.

Tenopyr, M. L. (1977). Content-construct confusion. *Personnel Psychology, 30,* 47-54.

Tenopyr, M. L., & Oeltjen, P. D. (1982). Personnel selection and classification. *Annual Review of Psychology, 33,* 581-618.

Thorndike, R. L. (1966). Reliability. In A. Anastasi (Ed.), *Testing problems in perspective.* Washington, DC: American Council on Education.

Thorndike, R. L., & Hagen, E. (1970). *Tests y técnicas de medición en psicología y educación.* Mexico City: Trillas.

Thorndike, R. L., & Hagen, E. (1977). *Measurement and evaluation in psychology and education* (4th ed.). New York: John Wiley.

Tous, J. M. (1986). Concepto y método de la psicologíe de la personalidad: apuntes para una puntualización teórica. *Buletin de Psicología, 13,* 33-42.

Tous, J. M. (1989). Modificación de conducta, personalidad y psicología clínica. *Análisis y Modificación de Conducta, 15,* 221-237.

Turkat, I. D. (1982). Behavior-analytic considerations of alternative clinical approaches. In P. L. Wachtel (Ed.), *Resistance: Psychodynamic and behavioral approaches.* New York: Plenum.

Turkat, I. D. (1988). Issues in the relationship between assessment and treatment. *Journal of Psychopathology and Behavioral Assessment, 10,* 185-197.

Turkat, I. D., & Meyer, V. (1982). The behavior-analytic approach. In P. L. Wachtel (Ed.), *Resistance: Psychodynamic and behavioral approaches.* New York: Plenum.

Twardosz, S., Schwartz, S., Fox, J., & Cunningham, J. L. (1979). Development and evaluation of a system to measure affectionate behavior. *Behavioral Assessment, 1,* 177-190

Uebersax, J. S. (1988). Validity inferences from interobserver agreement. *Psychological Bulletin, 104,* 405-416.

Ullmann, L. P., & Krasner, L. (Eds.) (1965). *Case studies in behavior modification.* New York: Holt, Rinehart & Winston.

Vernon, P. E. (1966). The concept of validity in personality studies. In B. Semeonoff (Ed.), *Personality assessment: Selected readings.* London: Penguin. (Original work published 1964)

Vizcarro, C. (1987). Aproximaciones empíricas al estudio del proceso diagnóstico. *Evaluación Psicológica/Psychological Assessment, 3,* 299-344.

Voeltz, L. M., & Evans, I. M. (1982). The assessment of behavioral interrelationships in clinical behavior therapy. *Behavioral Assessment, 4,* 131-165.

Wade, T. C., Baker, T. B., & Hartmann, D. P. (1979). Behavior therapists' self-reported views and practices. *Behavior Therapist, 2,* 3-6.

Wahler, R. G., & Fox, J. J. (1981). Setting events in applied behavior analysis: Toward a conceptual and methodological expansion. *Journal of Applied Behavior Analysis, 14,* 327-338.

Wallace, J. (1966). An abilities conception of personality: Some implications for personality measurement. *American Psychologist, 21,* 132-138.

Weiner, I. B. (1972). Does psychodiagnosis have a future? *Journal of Personality Assessment, 36,* 534-546.

Weiner, I. B. (1983). The future of psychodiagnosis revisited. *Journal of Personality Assessment, 47,* 451-459.

Weiss, D. J., & Davison, M. L. (1981). Test theory and methods. *Annual Review of Psychology, 32,* 629-658.

Weiss, R. L. (1968). Operant conditioning techniques in psychological assessment. In P. McReynolds (Ed.), *Advances in psychological assessment* (Vol. 1). Palo Alto, CA: Science & Behavior.

Wernimont, P. F., & Campbell, J. P. (1968). Signs, samples, and criteria. *Journal of Applied Psychology, 52,* 372-376.

Wessberg, H. W., Mariotto, M. J., Conger, A. J., Farrell, A. D., & Conger, J. C. (1979). Ecological validity of role plays for assessing heterosocial anxiety and skills of male college students. *Journal of Consulting and Clinical Psychology, 47,* 525-535.

Westmeyer, H. (1972). *Logik der Diagnostik: Grundlagen einer normativen Diagnostik.* Stuttgart: Kohlhammer.

Westmeyer, H. (1975). Zur Beziehung zwischen Verhaltensdiagnose und Verhaltenstherapie. *Psychologische Rundschau, 26,* 282-288.

Westmeyer, H. (1979). Wissenschaftstheoretische Grundlagen der Einzelfallanalyse. In F. Petermann & F. J. Hehl (Eds.), *Einzelfallanalyse.* Munich: Urban & Schwarzenberg.

Westmeyer, H. (1984). Diagnostik und therapeutische Entscheidung: Begründungsprobleme. In G. Jüttemann (Ed.), *Neue aspekte Klinisch-psychologischer Diagnostik.* Göttingen: Hogrefe.

Wiggins, J. S. (1973). *Personality and prediction: Principles of personality assessment.* Reading, MA: Addison-Wesley.

Wittenborn, J. R. (1957). The theory and technique of assessment. *Annual Review of Psychology, 8,* 331-356.

Witzlack, G. (1974). Theoretische und praktische Probleme der Konstruktion und An-wendung psychodiagnostischer Verfahren. In H. R. Boettcher, A. Seeber, & G. Witzlack (Eds.), *Psychodiagnostik—Probleme, Methoden, Ergebnisse*. Berlin: VEB.

Wolf, M. M. (1978). Social validity: The case for subjective measurement or: How applied behavior analysis is finding its heart. *Journal of Applied Behavior Analysis, 11,* 203-214.

Wolpe, J. (1969). *The practice of behavior therapy*. London: Pergamon.

Wolpe, J. (1977). Inadequate behavior analysis: The Achilles heel of outcome research in behavior therapy. *Journal of Behavior Therapy and Experimental Psychiatry, 8,* 1-3.

Wolpe, J. (1986). Individualization: The categorical imperative of behavior therapy practice. *Journal of Behavior Therapy and Experimental Psychiatry, 17,* 145-153.

Wolpe, J. (1989). The derailment of behavior therapy: A tale of conceptual misdirection. *Journal of Behavior Therapy and Experimental Psychiatry, 20,* 3-15.

Wolpe, J., & Turkat, I. D. (1985). Behavioral formulation of clinical cases. In I. D. Turkat (Ed.), *Behavioral case formulation*. New York: Plenum.

Yates, A. J. (1975). *Theory and practice of behavior therapy*. New York: John Wiley.

Ziskin, J. (1986). The future of clinical assessment. In B. S. Plake & J. C. Witt (Eds.), *The future of testing*. Hillsdale NJ: Lawrence Erlbaum.

AUTHOR INDEX

SUBJECT INDEX

157

ABOUT THE AUTHOR

Fernando Silva is Chair Professor at the University of Madrid, Spain. He received a Ph.D. from the University of Munich in 1975, a Ph.D. from the University of Madrid in 1977, and a Psy.D. from the University of Valencia in 1989. He has held teaching positions at the University of Chile; the Catholic University of Chile; the Max-Planck Institute of Psychiatry, Department of Psychology, Munich; and the University of Valencia. He is currently an executive committee member of the European Association of Psychological Assessment, Division II, Psychological Assessment of the International Association of Applied Psychology. He is also Editor-in-Chief of the *European Journal of Psychological Assessment*. His publications include 4 books in Spanish and 15 tests and more than 50 articles in Spanish, English, and German.

Made in the USA
Middletown, DE
13 February 2019